John Shand is a professional writer and musician.

Tony Wellington has worked in the film industry as script writer, director, first assistant director and editor and has lectured in filmcraft.

DON'T SHOOT THE BEST BOY!
THE FILM CREW AT WORK

John Shand & Tony Wellington

CURRENCY PRESS ● SYDNEY

First published in 1988
by Currency Press Pty Ltd,
PO Box 452
Paddington
N.S.W. 2021, Australia

Copyright© John Shand and Tony Wellington 1988

National Library of Australia
Cataloguing-in-Publication data
Shand, John, 1955-   .
Don't shoot the best boy!

ISBN 086819 219 8
    1. Motion pictures — Production and
    direction. 2. Cinematography.
    I. Wellington, Tony, 1955-   .
    II. Title

                    791.43'023

Designed by Debra Brash
Cover illustration by Tony Wellington.

Typeset by Post Typesetters, Brisbane
Printed by Southwood Press, Sydney

Published with the assistance of the Australian Film Commission.

Acknowledgements

This book was produced with the financial assistance of the Australian Film Commission. We would also like to thank Jim Sheldon, Sue Milliken, Colorfilm Pty Ltd, Judy Ditter, Vicki Harper and Hilary Linstead and Associates, the general reference staff at the State Library of NSW, the Australian Film and Television School Library, John Barry Rentals Company, Ian Gracie, Mark Zagar, Geoff Wharton, Nisey Ladmore, Greg Ricketson, and all those who kindly gave their time to be interviewed.

Contents

Contents

Introduction

Filmmaking is a collaborative art. Australian filmmaking has evolved in a manner that differs slightly from its overseas counterparts, and this is reflected in the duties of many of the crew. There is substantially less demarcation between individual roles in this country — a situation which, happily, has resulted in a more close-knit and amicable film community, and a greater degree of work-sharing and collaboration.

Inevitably, the high-risk, high-profile, high-cost-business of film-making takes place under extreme pressure, with time and money always at a premium. Chance also plays a part in the process. It is partly to overcome the vagaries of chance that every single member of the crew is directly involved in the decision-making process.

To keep proceedings practical rather than theoretical, anecdotal rather than academic, each chapter in the book is based on interviews with leading exponents of a given crew position. From the vast number of jobs on a feature film crew, thirteen have been selected for close scrutiny. As these roles are basically heads of departments, most of the other crew positions receive a mention during the discussions. In addition, we have provided an outline of every role on a feature film as an appendix, together with a glossary of technical terms in common use. Now, at last, the reader can find out what a best boy actually does, and what a clapper board is used for.

Don't Shoot the Best Boy! presents the scriptwriter first, though it should be pointed out that many films begin as an idea spawned by a producer or director, who then engages a writer to script it. The chapter on directors has been left until last as it helps to tie up the strands: having gained an understanding of the various crew roles, the final chapter provides insight not merely into what the director does, but how he or she may rely on the other collaborators. Actors bring an enormous amount of skill and creativity to a film but they have been excluded because their work is at first sight, more visible than that of the people behind the camera. Also, many of the books relating to film deal with the acting fraternity.

Although the material we are presenting relates largely to cinema feature films, the crews also tend to work on those television dramas which are shot on film (rather than video), with the roles and responsibilities being identical. Accordingly, a large number of TV mini-series are mentioned.

Naturally enough, the people we spoke to tended to highlight the importance of their own role's contribution to the finished film. Conflicting claims of responsibility — between a production designer and a director of photography, for example — should not be seen as a source of confusion: they merely reflect the areas of responsibility where two or more roles overlap, and also the enthusiasm with which most Australian crew members approach their craft.

The quoted material is derived entirely from interviews conducted by both authors specifically for this book. All of the interviewees were responsive to the aims of the book, and many were excited by the opportunity of having their contribution in the filmmaking process formally acknowledged.

We were struck by the wide variety of personalities among the interviewees. As cinematographer Peter James noted during his interview: 'The wonderful thing about a film crew is that you have so many diverse people. Yet they can all come together and be one family, live in one another's pockets for months on end, and all get along famously. I think it's incredible.'

The main purpose of this book is to provide some insight into how films are made, and what kind of people make them. It is about the hard-nosed, resilient and often bizarre nature of filmmaking in Australia. While it is not a manual of filmmaking techniques, it will certainly be of interest to the budding filmmaker and the working professional. It should also be illuminating for the armchair film buff and any student of Australian cinema. Most importantly, we wish to show how, at its best, this popular art form reflects a unique collaborative interaction between all its contributors.

John Shand
Tony Wellington
September, 1988

NOTE: The roles on a film crew may be filled by men or women, and to indicate this, in each chapter the editors have first referred to 'he or she'. Subsequently, the usual form 'he' is used where gender is not specified.

Scriptwriter David Williamson. *Photo by Jim Sheldon.*

1

Blank Page to Blueprint

THE WRITER

W hether a writer hammers out a screenplay of his or her own volition or is commissioned to do so by a producer, no film project really exists until there is a script.

'I think the writer is much more creatively reponsible for a film than the director,' said producer Matt Carroll. Often it is their sheer starting-with-a-blank-page creativity that makes a project happen.'

The prestige David Williamson has earned as a playwright places him in a unique position among Australian screen writers. The advertisements and posters which accompanied the release of *Travelling North* proclaimed it as 'A story by David Williamson', yet even he is somewhat bewildered by the lack of acknowledgement writers seem to receive from filmgoers and critics alike.

'It never ceases to amaze me that thematic parallels are drawn through a director's body of work that obviously are not there. The film theorists are desperate to find constant thematic concerns in the work of directors who often use scripts by wildly different writers in wildly different areas. Certainly, it must be true that directors are attracted to a certain type of theme when they're reading scripts to see which one they will do, but beyond that, a lot of film theorising is spurious.

'I think it is because some people who want to regard film as an art think that art must be the work of one person. They can't conceive of an art which is at all collaborative. There has to be an artist, so it must be the director. Quite extraordinary!'

For David Williamson and writer Everett de Roche, the overwhelming proportion of their screenplays that have reached the cinema have been commissioned by a producer.

'I haven't tried writing an original screenplay since *Petersen*, filmed in 1974,' said Williamson, 'because it seems an extremely difficult enterprise. Most producers have their own ideas of what is going to work in the cinema, and their own projects. So it is very hard to write a screenplay on spec — to spend six months or so putting it down — then hawk it around dozens of producers to see if anyone is interested in doing it.'

Everett de Roche, on the other hand, continues to write unsolicited scripts whenever he has a few weeks to spare between projects.

'Maybe one in ten projects actually gets up, so you have to increase the odds somehow. Someone will eventually ask, "Have you got anything in the bottom drawer?" If the only thing you do is write scripts, you have to keep a number of irons in the fire. Very often work will come out of left field. *Patrick* was like that. It sat around for about three years, and then almost accidentally someone stumbled across the script, and wanted to develop it.'

The amount of detail a producer or director may give when briefing a writer varies tremendously. The source material may be an existing book or stage play, or it may just be an idea.

'Part of the reason for the producer coming to me', explained de Roche, 'is to come up with an approach, which I regard as the hardest part of the whole thing. If you come up with the right approach — which is mainly a matter of deciding where to start and where to finish the story — the actual drafting of the script can almost be painting by numbers. That's the easy part.

'Very often the novel you are handed is perhaps five hundred pages. There are about a hundred pages in a screenplay, so it means you are going to have to hack into it ruthlessly. I always start with great reverence for the novel, especially if it is something well known. I am usually fairly beguiled by the prose, and want to use as much of it as possible — if nothing else, just to see why it's *not* going to work that way. And also, sometimes, to prove to the producer — who, after all, has paid all this money for the copyright — why you have to change it radically; so that he can see it on paper and see why it doesn't work. A lot of things work perfectly well in a novel that don't work at all on the screen.

'I battled for years with a thing called *Naked Under Capricorn*, by Olaf Ruhen. That project has been around since the nineteen-fifties. Bette Davis had the copyright to it at one time. The main character is someone who does nothing throughout the whole book. He refers to himself as 'the culpable bystander' who stood around and did nothing while the Aboriginal race sort of caved in. That works wonderfully well in the book, but to have a protagonist in a movie who does nothing throughout the whole movie — it's a contradication in terms. The protagonist has to provoke action.'

David Williamson's films have been initiated by both producers and directors, often with considerable input during the writing.

'*Gallipoli* was Peter Weir's idea. He went to Gallipoli and had a feeling that he wanted to make a film about it. He got in touch with me before he had formulated much beyond that. I admired Peter's work and liked the thought of tackling Gallipoli as a subject. We worked together to develop a storyline, and then I wrote successive drafts of this on and off for four years. We took different tacks all the time. The early drafts were all of just about everyone who ever stepped onto the Gallipoli peninsula, and couldn't be shot because they were too expensive. Then it gradually got simpler and simpler over the years. I would do a draft, he'd criticise or give input, and finally we got something that somebody wanted to film.

'With *Phar Lap*, the producer John Sexton came to me with the idea that he wanted to make a film about the horse. He didn't have a director chosen for it. He needed a screenplay to interest a director. Initially I wasn't interested at all because I have no interest in horseracing whatsoever. But Sexton talked me into it. He was very fervent and enthusiastic about the project, and when he gave me the research material I saw that there was a lot of drama surrounding the horse, which I felt added up to a good story. The characters around Phar Lap interested me a lot: Tommy Woodcock, the one who loved the horse dearly as if it were a human being; Telford, the trainer, who thought the horse verified the fact that he was the greatest trainer in the world; and Davis, the businessman, who saw the horse as a money-making machine.

'With *Travelling North*, producer Ben Gannon just rang up one day and said, "I'd like to film that play of yours." He'd seen it a few years before at the Marion Street Theatre in Sydney and it had stuck in his mind. Although I'd had other approaches to do

Travelling North, I wasn't as convinced by them as I was by Ben, who I'd been with on *Gallipoli*. I thought he was a man of taste, and very straight. When he suggested Leo McKern to play Frank I thought it sounded terrific. We didn't have a director in the early stages, but I trusted Ben, and I had always thought that *Travelling North* had the potential to film well.'

The stepping stones on the way to a first draft vary according to the writer's methods and the demands of the producer or director. Everett de Roche likes to use cards on which he jots down his notes for the plot. These grow in number throughout the planning stage, and make restructuring as simple as shuffling the pack. They also let him move straight to a first draft, unless the producer demands a treatment.

'I'm not even sure what a treatment is, there are so many different sorts. It can be anything from the writer's own notes which at a fairly rough stage he shares with the director and producer, all the way to a very polished fifty or seventy-five page document that is actually a selling document: money is either going to be raised or not raised on the strength of it. Now, that is very difficult to do. It has to read like a short story, and it has to be all things to all people, because you have no idea who is going to be reading it and making decisions.

'Whether or not the project gets up might depend on your prose, and really, script writing shouldn't have much to do with prose. I find that very demanding. Very often, a producer will say, "Just knock out five pages." That's even harder. It is easier to do fifty pages than to do five pages. A five page document that you know is going to a reader at Universal Studios in Los Angeles is something I might spend two weeks on — to get those five pages just right. Because if they're not right, you don't get a second chance.

'If a producer insists on going through these stages, then I'll go through them. Otherwise, I'll just prepare the thing myself, using various systems, including those cards. But they're certainly not in any form that anyone else would understand. They're just for me.'

Williamson also prefers to bypass treatments, going directly from a rough outline to a first draft:

'I find treatments very bloodless things that can often inhibit creativity. A treatment is just an abridged first draft, without the dialogue which is the most interesting part of it. Once I know what the story is, by virtue of an outline, I want to actually write out in full what the characters are doing and saying to each other.

'The contract time for a first draft is usually about twelve weeks. You can do a very racy rough draft in six weeks or so, and then spend a fair bit of time hacking it and chopping it on your word processor — refining it and getting it a bit better before it goes in as the official first draft.'

In the case of *The Year of Living Dangerously*, Williamson's first draft came after two other writers had already attempted screenplays. Christopher Koch, whose novel the film was based on, had worked on a screenplay with Peter Weir, but their efforts proved unsatisfactory. An American writer had then wrung three further drafts from the concept, which were no closer to what Weir was after. It was at this point that Williamson was called in, to see what he could make of the material. The Koch/Weir draft was used as a launching pad — the American writer's efforts being dumped altogether. Williamson's frustrations with *Living Dangerously* went beyond the complications of being the third writer to work on it.

'It was a very difficult project, inherently. There had to be a balance between the Billy Kwan character — played by Linda Hunt — including that character's compassion for the starving people of the Third World, against the love affair between Mel Gibson and Sigourney Weaver. Structurally, the two things don't sit very easily. If you really get into the Billy Kwan character, and have the audience feeling stirred and emotional about the plight of the Third World, then it's hard to really justify the interest in whether Mel Gibson and Sigourney Weaver get off together.'

This problem was exacerbated once shooting had begun, when Peter Weir required some further rewriting.

'Linda proved to be such a captivating character that Peter wanted to use her more, so there was some rewriting: more material for Linda, and slightly less for the other characters. But sometimes things like that can throw the structural balance out of kilter, and I felt we never quite got a balance between those two things.

'I wanted a little bit more depth and insight into the relationship between Mel and Sigourney. It was just a matter of a couple of scenes — not anything huge. But who's to say who was right? I still believe my suggestions would have been better for the film, but who knows? They were never shot, so it is easy for me to sit back and say, "I had the solution, but nobody listened".'

Unless a project is initiated by its director, the writer must look toward the producer for feedback on the earliest drafts, until a director is appointed. Both de Roche and Williamson crave maximum feedback between drafts, whomever it comes from. On *Patrick* and *Roadgames*, de Roche enjoyed working with Richard Franklin, who was both director and co-producer.

'Richard comes in very early on a project, and rings me every day, almost like a nagging wife. But I prefer that amount of involvement. To have a director involved that early in the project is great, because he is the best possible script editor. He is the one who has to go out and actually shoot the thing, and if he says a scene is going to play okay, then you can have faith in that.

'In the absence of a director, which is in the case of most projects, I would like to get more feedback from a producer. I find producers, by and large, really don't have the energy that it takes to get involved. They have too many other things to worry about. They don't want to know the details of how you are going to structure the story, and all of that. Even a lot of directors don't want to know about the project until you've got a final script. So I would prefer to have a nagging producer who is always on your back, because at least you know they are still alive, and haven't gone bankrupt.

'I might do half a dozen drafts before I call it a first draft, and pass it on to a producer. They read the script, and have a certain amount of time to get back to you with revisions, and then you have a certain amount of time to respond to that with a second draft, and so forth.

'Some producers might take the time to write out fifteen pages of very detailed notes referring to scene numbers and page numbers. Others will just make half a dozen comments along the lines of "fix this" and "fix that". That procedure goes on and on, sometimes into filming. By that stage, you are usually revising for the director rather than the producer.

'That is another thing. You might do a number of drafts to please a particular producer, who then brings a director on board who sees things completely differently. He or she will invariably want to put a personal stamp on it somehow.

'I think the success or failure of the movie can very often be to what degree the relationship with the director has been built up, and has worked. What you really do in a script is just write notes to the director — try to communicate an idea. If the two of you can become one on that idea, then that is terrific. Because Richard Franklin worked so closely with me, for instance, there can be no mistake that we're on the same wavelength. That's story-wise. When it gets to the style of direction, that's another thing completely, and I might do things differently from the way he would.

But as far as the preparation of the script is concerned, he's been terrific.'

For David Williamson, feedback from the producer and/or the director is essential, simply because they are the ones who both spend the money, and who are responsible for putting the product on the screen.   •

'I think I'm genuinely past the days when I'd throw up my hands in horror at any adverse criticism. I'm so thoroughly used to everybody having their input that it doesn't worry me, as long as they leave me to go away and think about it myself afterwards. As a rule I work on that input, even if I don't accept it all as being true.

'They are usually general comments, like, "The second half of the script flags", "The female character seems a little recessive", "That area of the character seems to be unmotivated", or, "The coincidence is unlikely". Comments about when the story loses interest, impetus, or believability: those three areas are usually the ones that are spotted accurately by good producers and directors. Usually, the solution is left to you.

'Sometimes there will be a specific suggestion like, "What if she had a sister, and that sister did that?" Structure is so complex. You start with a blank page, and a million ways to go at the end of every line you have written. There can be endless debate and endless argument about which is the best structure for this particular story. With good directors and producers, the debate is usually fairly succinct, within those three broad areas.'

Trusted people may read a draft at the producer's request, to gather further opinions.

'If a good producer says that X, Y and Z have all read it', continued Williamson, 'and that they think the second half really runs out of steam, then you ignore that sort of comment at your peril. Their ambition is to ensure that a film grips and holds an audience. If they are all convinced it doesn't, then it is wise to have another look at it. Sometimes you disagree, and think, "You just haven't seen what's going to happen when a certain casting takes place there".

'I think all the scripts I have worked on have been altered to some degree by input of that general nature. Certainly, the drafts of *Gallipoli* varied wildly, from a huge panoramic film involving a cast of thousands, down finally to a simple story of two lads. So Peter's influence on the story was certainly strong in that one. At a middling stage, when suddenly they said, "Look, it can't be done with a cast of thousands", Peter had the brain-wave of starting the story off a lot later. He cut and pasted one of my old scripts, wrote some rough dialogue, and that was the basis for the next draft I did.'

When a director has yet to be appointed, both writers like the producer to consult them on the choice. Ideally, this consultancy extends into the casting stage. Williamson:

'On *Phar Lap*, the producer and director had me in to see all the casting video tapes, and there was one crucial choice where they were heading for a major miscast. Sometimes at an early stage, the writer can see the characters and their characteristics more clearly than anyone else. Film is so fragile that you only need one major miscast and the film is blown. Many of the failures in the film industry that have been blamed on the script have, to my eyes, been very competent scripts, but they have been absolutely killed by casting that hasn't brought out the possibilities inherent in the relationships within the script.'

Once a film has been cast, and any rehearsals or script readings commence, there is considerable scope for three-way interaction between writer, actors and director.

'If the director is happy, and doesn't feel threatened', Williamson said, 'and the cast doesn't feel threatened — which they usually don't — I think the rehearsals are the time to do any tinkering if there is something to be done. Even if I'm not there fulltime I can be on call. If a scene is not working and the director says to come and have a look at it, I'm only too happy to do that. But I don't like breathing over the director's shoulder when he or she is working with the cast.

'Sometimes, after a couple of weeks of rehearsal they'll be tempted to change the script because they have heard these lines of yours so many times that they are getting bored with them. They think they will come up with some new ones which sound more interesting — and probably do the first time you hear them. But the audience of a film is only going to hear that line once. In most cases, you are right and the actors are wrong, because when you've written hundreds of thousands of lines that actors have said, you get a feeling for which work and which don't. So if there are any changes, I like to be informed, and I like to argue the case against it. If I think they are right, I'll go along with them. I'm not inflexible.

If they come up with a better way of handling a scene, I'll be only too happy to rewrite it.'

For de Roche, the coming together of a director and actors also precipitates another set of revisions.

'That's all part of the service as far as I'm concerned. I expect to tailor the script not only to the director, but to the lead actors: to make everyone as happy as possible with the script.'

He finds rehearsals an infrequent luxury. A more common procedure on his projects is to make do with a reading by the actors.

'It's a good chance to sort things out a bit, and get to know each other. If the actor has any problems with the character, that is when he or she should speak up. The more involved I am, the more rewriting there is, I think. Having the writer there to actually do the work probably encourages people to come forward with ideas. Very often, those ideas are terrific, so I'm happy to incorporate them.'

This process can spill over into the actual shooting period, too.

'I've got shooting scripts where some of the scenes are pencilled in on the back of a page: rewritten half an hour before the scene was shot, which can be terrific — it can be spontaneous and all of that — or it can be disastrous.

'Often, you'll imagine one character to be unsympathetic, then you start watching rushes, and he's coming across sympathetically. There is nothing you can do, except to exploit that, and make it work. That means going back to the script and looking at the scenes that haven't been shot yet, in order to make that character conform more with what we are seeing on the screen.'

The writer does not really have a function on set, and producers are loath to pay for their presence. Generally this suits Williamson and de Roche quite well.

'If the producer wanted me to be there all the time, I could get them round an awful lot of problems', said de Roche. 'It is easy to save $10,000 by running a page through the typewriter, if I know what the problems are. But I really object when they try to fix it themselves and do a bad job of it.

'They had a radical change to the story in *Harlequin*, and I was in Mexico and couldn't be contacted. I'd written the story as a sort of updated version of *Rasputin*, with Rasputin turned into a Catholic priest. The film had been financed and they were ready to go when they got cold feet about alienating the Catholics or something, and didn't want to make him a priest. They just took out that whole aspect of the character, which left a huge void. If he's not a priest, then what is he? But I couldn't really complain, because I wasn't here to do anything about it, or I would have fought to keep it as it was. Failing that, I would have tried to come up with an alternative that still got across the same idea.'

Another of de Roche's scripts which required unexpected surgery during the shoot was a project which was crammed full of action and stunts.

'I don't like to write something that can't be done, so I had checked out all the locations, and checked things out with the stunt man. I had continually gone back to the producer to say, "Look, are you certain we can do this? This is going to be a big stunt", and so forth, and was told repeatedly, "Don't worry about it. That's not the writer's domain. You just write". Famous last words.

'They got several weeks into filming and I got an urgent message to join them. They were running out of money, and it was handed to me to fix, which more or less meant rewriting the whole last half of the script in about two days; taking out all the big stunts and stuff which were to be the climax of the film. As a result, you can tell almost to the frame in the movie where they ran out of money. That is one where I screamed and hollered, but there's not much you can do. It's a case of either I radically revise the script, or someone else is going to come along and radically revise it. That is an extreme example. Usually it's a matter of a line here and there.'

David Williamson has been lucky enough not to encounter an economic need for major script revisions during a shoot.

'I really don't go for the seat-of-the-pants model of filmmaking. Especially not when you are spending ten million dollars. It's stupid and criminal. It's amateursville.'

Leaving tampering with the script aside, the director obviously has an impact on the writer's work as an inevitable result of translating the screenplay on to celluloid. A common critical view is that directors are interpreters of the script, but the extent of this interpretation varies tremendously.

Five of Williamson's films — *Stork* (directed by Tim Burstall), *The Removalists* (Tom Jeffrey), *Travelling North* (Carl Schultz), *Don's Party* and *The Club* (both Bruce Beresford) — had past lives as successful stage plays. This left less scope than usual for directorial input at the scripting stage, and generally made it difficult for the directors to use these projects as the basis for an *auteur*'s statement, even if they had wanted to.

'With *Phar Lap*', said Williamson, 'I think that Simon Wincer just wanted to bring a stylish visual feel to a script that he was happy with. He certainly had input during the script stage, but he didn't want to centre the film on his own personal feelings or obsessions, because essentially he came to the script after it was written. I mean, we did further drafts, but it was there and existing.

'I think Peter Weir certainly has that *auteur* approach to film. I think he likes the script to reflect his own personal obsessions to some degree. I suppose, particularly in *Living Dangerously*, I did feel some tension with Peter, because you do feel more like a functionary in a situation like that. But, to be fair, once the script was finalised in both *Gallipoli* and *The Year of Living Dangerously*, Peter adhered very closely to it. But he had strong input through the script stages. He said to me, "Look, I'm a director, but I'm not a writer. My skills of characterisation and dialogue are not as great as I'd like them to be. That's why you're here".'

Interpretation may not be a strong enough term to describe the way first-time feature director Russell Mulcahy dealt with de Roche's film, *Razorback*.

'I had written the script as an action-thriller, and Russell, being very sort of stylised, had a completely different approach to the look of the film. It is bizarre in places — it's sort of like a rock clip. You almost expect Elton John to leap out and do a number, or something. Now if I'd known what his style was going to be, I could have written for that style, and I think the thing would have worked much better. It is inherent in Russell's style that anything he did would have his stamp.'

While the writer has no specific role on set, both de Roche and Williamson have looked in on proceedings.

'Unless the writer has a specific title on the set', said de Roche, 'I find it's really awkward. On *Frog Dreaming*, I wasn't just the writer, I was a co-producer, and that made all the difference. So that was quite a different experience — quite enjoyable. I was there for a great deal of time.'

'I do like to go along and see a bit of the shoot', Williamson commented, 'if it doesn't worry the director or the cast; but not too much of it. I was up in Port Douglas on *Travelling North* for three or four days, which was terrific. I had no great function. I mean, I might have rewritten a word or two, but the main thing was just to look at the film being shot. If you have a good cast, and they're doing it well, there's nothing much you can do at that stage. So I was quite relaxed.'

An analysis of these writers' techniques is not really the province of this book, although de Roche was vehement on the subject of script length and its ramifications for a production:

'I'm always trying to write the elusive ninety-minute screenplay. Ninety minutes is perfect in my opinion. But the producers go, "Oh! Ninety pages!" Almost as if they are not quite getting their money's worth unless it's a hundred and twenty or a hundred and fifty pages. It is really hard to convince them that less is better. Less is also much more difficult. It would be easy to write a great rambling three-hundred-page screenplay, which *Patrick*, my first movie, was — completely undisciplined. If I was to go back and look at those three hundred pages, I would recognise a lot of indulgences.

'In *Razorback*, we went with a script that was too long. I could sense when I was writing it that things were going to have to be cut. There's a temptation by the director and producer to say, "Let's go with this, and we will look at it in rushes, and start cutting then." But because of the pace you're working at by that stage, it's just too easy to make criticial mistakes. What seems like a great idea when you're watching rushes can be disastrous later. So I like to make my scripts as lean as possible. I am becoming really fanatical about getting it down to the right time.'

Occasionally he writes camera shots into the script when he feels it makes a contribution.

'I haven't run across any directors who have said, "Don't do that." They all seem to appreciate your opinion. I'll usually try to avoid calling the shot, but make it obvious: "His hand grabs the pen" suggests a close-up without actually having to say it. But sometimes just stating, for example, a helicopter shot, simply saves time. Usually, a director will appreciate that rather than resent it, and they will, of course, be free to change it any way they like. I suppose I see it first as an image, and then all the rest of the work is trying to communicate that image to somebody else.'

'I don't try and dictate a visual style or anything like that', Williamson said. 'I see my role as a screenwriter as constructing story, character, and dialogue. The basic thrust — the reason I am a writer — is that I want to tell stories. I want to find characters that are interesting, and doing interesting things.

'I think cinema at its best is another way of telling a story; preferably a story about human interaction. I don't see cinema as a series of moving paintings. It is a curious art form, because it's stranded somewhere in between. I used to go to film festivals dutifully as a youth, and was often bored by beautiful films that took an eternity to tell a story. I do think a lot of Australian films have suffered because they haven't been well written, and the reason is that writers haven't written them. I think there are a few genuine writer/directors, but there aren't many, because it is just such an enormous fluke if you have skills in two disparate areas.'

With this perspective, it is hardly surprising that David Williamson is only vaguely tempted to try his hand at directing:

'It's not a mad obsession. I'm not driven to do it, because in general I've been lucky in getting pretty good directors to work on my scripts. I' mean, the motivation hasn't been: "Someone has absolutely ruined a masterpiece of mine. Next time I've got to do it myself". I've never felt like that. I think my skills are in the writing area, and I always seem to be too busy writing these days to even contemplate the thought of taking nine months off to get a film born. It's a long haul, and I think a director has to be a fairly psychologically tough character to cope with all the vicissitudes during that nine months. I'm not sure I've got that kind of temperament. I think I'm happier sitting in front of my word-processor, dreaming up the blueprint that someone else will later do.'

De Roche directed a sequence in *Frog Dreaming*, and is keen to try again.

'Directing is probably the next logical step for a writer to take. I would certainly like to direct at least one film and then see what happens after that. I've never really been a hundred percent satisfied with anything of my own that I've seen on the screen. I think that by directing, I would find out why it doesn't come out that way, or else I would be able to do it the way I'd intended, and make a point.'

Any disappointment in the end product begs the question of where the satisfaction lies in writing for the screen. David Williamson is pleased if he feels his areas — characterisation, dialogue, structure — are working.

'I think Beresford did a very good job on *Don's Party*, and as good as he could do on *The Club*, which was less amenable to film, I think. I still think we got the overall structure right on *Gallipoli*.

The whole running theme — one running to his death, the other running to try and save him — works, so I'm very happy with that one.

'I was very pleased with *Phar Lap*, despite all my initial doubts. Simon Wincer was very competent, and shot the script that we wrote. I was pleased with *Travelling North*. I think Carl did a very sensitive job in getting that on to celluloid. The performances he encouraged out of that cast were terrific. Apart from minor and non-acrimonious disagreements — the few lines he should have left in that he cut out — I was very pleased.'

'It's hard to know when to let go of a project' observed de Roche, 'when to say, "Yeah, this is finished to the best of my ability". I can always see things that I would like to change and polish a bit more. I guess what pleases me is the response of others, especially when it comes from someone on a film crew, because those guys have seen everything. For one of them to come up and say, "This is a bit different. I was looking forward to this" — that, I really think, is a big compliment. I suppose you're writing to please others. If they're pleased, I'm pleased.'

Producer Jane Scott. *Photo by Jim Sheldon.*

2

From Conception to Release

THE PRODUCER

I f the filmmaking machine is seen as a hierarchical pyramid, then the producer is its apex. Ultimately it is the producer who ensures that the film gets made.

Although he or she is committed to a film from its inception until long after the rest of the crew has moved on to other projects, the producer's role is much less tangible. The resurgent Australian film industry has spawned a remarkable assortment of producers, some of whom — such as Matt Carroll, Jane Scott and Tony Buckley — have served long apprenticeships in filmmaking, while others have had no practical experience of film at all. Accordingly, their approaches to the role of producer are as diverse as their backgrounds.

This chapter is primarily concerned with the contribution of those people who receive 'producer' credits, but there are also executive producers, line producers, co-producers, and associate producers. While none of these has a hard and fast definition, we can at least shade in the general area covered by each title.

The executive producer is commonly responsible for raising finance. They may also be someone appointed by investors to keep tabs on the producer, or someone who personally invests a large sum, in return for which they ask for their name to be in large letters on the screen. Generally speaking, however, an executive producer is a bit of a wheeler-dealer or high-powered business executive; someone who makes ultimate decisions about major matters. They usually raise the necessary capital to make the film, and have direct dealings with the investors. Not all films have executive producers, however.

In recent years, Matt Carroll has shifted his focus from producing to executive producing. He now oversees several projects simultaneously, through the production company Roadshow, Coote and Carroll, and employs individual producers for each project. His participation as executive producer extends to choosing projects, employing writers and directors, and keeping an eye on casting decisions. By the time a film is in the final stages of pre-production, much of his involvement is complete, and he is busy developing other projects.

A line producer may be employed by an experienced producer who is too busy to deal with day-to-day business, or by an inexperienced producer who wishes to maintain creative control, but doesn't know the basic *modus operandi* of filmmaking. In the latter situation, Jane Scott filled this role on *Crocodile Dundee*.

'John Cornell and Paul Hogan didn't particularly want to do the nuts and bolts part of it', she explained, 'because they didn't have any feature film experience.' She deferred to Cornell, the producer, for any decision she felt had to be made by him, but, nonetheless, was essentially running the production.

For *Crocodile Dundee II*, Scott became co-producer with Cornell, who also directed, with the result that much more of the producer's responsibility fell on her shoulders.

Associate producers are the chameleons of the film industry. He or she may be someone who is brought in to assist a flagging production and sort out a mess. The term may even be doled out as a pay-off or favour to someone who has absolutely nothing to do with producing the film. In some cases the associate producer actually fulfills the role of a line producer for an inept or lazy producer, or the role of production manager on a higher salary. Jane Scott:

'My first associate producing job was with Bruce Beresford on *Barry McKenzie Holds His Own*. He was directing it, Reg Grundy was financing it, and I was production managing. Because we had worked together for so long, I guess Bruce wanted me to have more control. It wasn't a matter of producing it, because he was really doing that. But being associate producer gave me more control over the finances and the production. I wasn't so much working *for* the production as supervising it. It was management.'

Traditionally, producers are thought of as the people in charge of the money: finding the finances and overseeing them. Raising money for films is a very time-consuming and trying process. Producers must be familiar with finance brokerage, government legislation on film funding, and the whole economic climate, which is no easy task when all of these areas are apt to change from one moment to the next.

The Australian film industry is presently undergoing dramatic upheavals, largely as a result of changes to film financing. The Federal Government's tax incentive scheme known as 10B(A), which offers substantial savings for investors in film, is being phased out. In its place, direct funding will go to a 'film bank' to be called the Film Finance Corporation, which will invest in what it deems commercially viable films. For producers, this now means having to convince the board of the film bank that their project is likely to realise a return on its investment. Both parties may also seek to bolster the bank's investment with private money. The less attractive alternatives to film bank funding include the difficult task of raising all the budget from private sources, or securing some sort of co-production deal with an overseas film company. Government film bodies, in particular the Australian Film Commission, will continue to fund films at the development stage, and hopefully also fund less commercial, experimental, and low-budget features.

A pre-sale — a deal with a distribution company which guarantees to purchase the distribution rights for an agreed sum — often has to be secured in order to attract investors. (This may prove to be equally necessary to gain film bank funding.) Securing pre-sales can also take up a great deal of the producer's time and energy, long before a project is given the green light. Pre-sales are addressed in more detail, later in this chapter.

'The easiest and most pleasant job for me is the making of the film', said Jane Scott. 'It is something that I revel in, and that I have been trained to do. The more unpleasant aspect of the job is certainly the money-raising. I'm not a financial wizard, so I don't talk sophisticated money deals with potential investors, but I do hire people who can help do that. It's not the part of the job that I relish, but it is a part you have to get involved in. Even on productions where I'm a hired hand, I will get involved in different ways, because it is all part of what has to be done. On *Crocodile*

Dundee, for example, I was involved with the accountant in putting together the prospectus to attract potential investors.'

The most successful, and arguably the better Australian producers, are those with a good grounding in the medium, giving them a thorough grasp of filmmaking principles. This would seem to be imperative if a producer is to collaborate effectively at a creative level. Jane Scott again:

'You need to be able to talk to people on *their* level about their job or their equipment. So many times I've seen producers who don't know anything about the different areas of production, so they are unable to explain what they want. They just don't know what is possible. I meet a lot of people who say they want to produce. I suppose it's a sort of pioneering spirit: they read a book or a script and think, "What's to stop me producing this? I want to see it on the screen".'

The producer's artistic input is in part determined by whether the project is considered a 'producer's picture' or a 'director's picture'. For example, *Caddie* was a producer's picture. It was Tony Buckley's idea to make the film, for which he sought out a writer to provide the screenplay, and then commissioned the director. *The Night the Prowler,* on the other hand, could be termed a director's picture. In this case the director, Jim Sharman, went in search of a producer, and approached Buckley, who agreed to do it.

On a producer's picture, the producer will begin with an idea, a storyline, or even a completed script, and proceed to realise his vision. This will include actually *casting* a director, and, if necessary, a scriptwriter who seems appropriate.

Not all films are clearly delineated as the producer's or director's, however. Although *Bliss* was initiated by Tony Buckley, he is inclined to attribute the film more to its director, Ray Lawrence. This is because it was very much Lawrence's conception of how to translate the book onto celluloid which determined the final effect.

All this points to the fact that a good producer knows when to take creative control, and when to support other people's creativity. The corollary is that one of their chief skills is being an excellent judge of other people's talents and abilities, and what will and will not work on the screen.

The first task on a new project is obviously to come up with a script. Writer David Williamson's dealings with some producers have occasionally left him less than impressed:

'One of the essential qualities of a producer is script sense and script editing sense. There are only a handful of producers who seem to have it. A lot of them think that scripting should be dealt with as quickly and cheaply as possible: if you can get a screenplay for $10,000, it is better than spending $30,000 on it. It's a mentality that sees all screenplays as equal, but the cheaper ones are a bargain.'

Of course a good producer will go to any lengths to ensure the quality of a script, as Matt Carroll did with *Breaker Morant*:

'An article on Morant by Kit Denton attracted me enormously, so I bought an option on his book and had a screenplay written, which was far too expensive. It would have cost millions of dollars to make in the days when we were working in tens of thousands.'

It transpired that Ken Ross had written a stage play, telling the story through the court martial. Carroll immediately saw that this was the way to go, and approached Ross about the rights to the play. As it turned out, Ross had already allowed David Stevens and Jonathon Hardy to create a screenplay out of it. Carroll chased them up, read the script, and knew he had found what he wanted.

'I was working with Bruce Beresford on finishing *Money Movers* at that time. I gave it to Bruce and asked him what he thought about it. He told me it'd make a terrific film, but that it needed further re-writes, because not all the flashbacks in it were working. I said that if I could get the money, would he do the re-writes and direct it, and he agreed.'

As well as chasing money, Carroll was also very much involved in the scripting process.

'Bruce and I worked in a very collaborative way, in that I story-edited most of *Breaker*, solving some of the tremendous structural problems we had. Bruce got sort of "written out" on it, we did so many drafts. It was a very complicated script to get right, because it was so difficult balancing the flashbacks with the courtroom drama.'

As an interesting aside, there was one scene in the screenplay which was never shot, through lack of funds.

'It was a pivotal scene, where you first meet Jack Thompson, and he's burning a Boer farmhouse', Carroll recounted. 'We had the location, but we just ran out of money. It was a great pity because, as the film is now, he just arrives in town, whereas before it opened with the burning farmhouse, and all these Boers and blacks being put into carts. Jack Thompson is standing there looking at it with disgust, when a soldier rides up and tells him he is needed to act for Morant and the others.'

'That interlinks with when he makes the great speech, and says, "Don't talk to me about justice. I've been burning people's homes", and, of course, you've seen him burning people's homes. The impact of that speech is now much less. It's a great pity, but we had to find something to cut.'

Another producer-initiated project was *Sunday Too Far Away*, which was born more or less by accident. Carroll and co-producer Gil Brearly had actually intended to make a movie about Gallipoli. They contracted John Dingwall to write the screenplay, but the project subsequently fell apart. During this time, Carroll and Dingwall found themselves sharing reminiscences of outback life: Carroll came from Coolah in the middle of NSW sheep country, and Dingwall had a brother-in-law who was a shearer. They decided to substitute a story about shearers, for the Gallipoli contract. Dingwall was packed off to Coolah to research the material, which resulted in his acclaimed original screenplay.

For *Stormboy*, Carroll read Colin Thiele's book, and decided it could be a hugely popular film with both children and adults. However, for it to be a feature, the story needed expanding:

'The first writer had the Aboriginal character suffering from tuberculosis, so I scrapped the whole lot and started again. A friend of mine recommended Sonia Borg, whom I went to meet. I knew she was the right person when I found she lived in a house full of animals. I suspect the first writer didn't like animals... You make those sorts of mistakes.

'So I found the book, and had the thing written. The visual concept for that film is mine: Henri Safran was a hired gun. The whole myth of the director — that one person creates the film — is just not honest, as far as I'm concerned. It has to be a collaborative thing. It is staggering that my name is never mentioned when I read about pictures I've produced, and yet I created those films.'

Frequently a writer approaches a producer with a script, as when Bob Ellis took *Goodbye Paradise* to Jane Scott.

'When I first read it', said Jane, 'I remember saying, "I've just got to make this". I was laughing at the script, it was so funny. But it was a very complicated story, and although the writing was funny, I knew it would be difficult to film.

'Both Bob and I very much wanted to work with Carl Schultz. I have a great respect for Carl's directing and storytelling. It wasn't a case of me saying how it should be: we would talk about the more difficult parts, and he'd usually have a good solution. The three of us talked about it bit by bit, and Bob went away and worked it over.

'With *Crocodile Dundee II*, John Cornell rang me and said, "We've finished the new script. How soon can we start the production?" It went through another one or two re-writes, but the story stayed the same. Paul Hogan wrote that one with his son, and we all discussed a few things. But Paul and John would take the comments, and maybe change some things and not others. This wasn't a situation in which you give an idea, and it hits the page clearly as your idea. It was very much Paul's show.'

The producer who initiates a project will try to 'cast' a director who will share that vision of how the film will be created, and be capable of executing it. Carroll:

'If you want to make a film like *Bliss*, you don't engage a director with ducks-on-the-wall taste. You can't expect him to go outside his own boundaries, so you need to know his other work. As you get more experienced, you choose the director more carefully for the subject that you are doing, so that you both end up making the same movie. That's what it is all about: everyone has to be making the same film, or otherwise you are just a production manager for the director, doing whatever he wants.'

Tony Buckley has taken some remarkably successful gambles on directors with no track record.

'Don't ask me how you make these decisions', he said. 'That's what Hollywood calls a gut reaction: you sense whether a person can do it or not. It's just another part of being a producer.

'In the case of *Bliss*, first of all the investors and the New South Wales Film Corporation had to get over their incredulity that anyone would want to make a film about this peculiar book. When we said that Ray Lawrence was going to direct it, "Who's Ray Lawrence?" was the response. I told them he'd only done television commercials, and they all thought I'd fallen off my twig.

'However, Ray had a formidable reputation as an art director of some nineteen years, and a TV commercials director of some fourteen years. The New South Wales Film Corporation said they'd go along with it, but we still needed to raise three and a half million dollars.

'So Ray had this idea: we chose a scene from *Bliss*, hired a 35 mm camera, and went off one Sunday to an old hotel in Double Bay. We used the actors who were to be in the film, and just put together what crew we could get. I went out to watch Ray shoot that sequence, and I felt totally confident, because he not only knew what he was doing, but he didn't fiddle around, taking hours to light and so on, like they do in commercials.

'We edited it on 35 mm, and put it to tape in a wide-screen format, so people would know it was film and not television. It was two and a half minutes long, and we pedalled that into town to the group of investors' representatives and the Corporation. They all looked at it, and not only did they begin to understand what the film was about, but they saw the man could direct.'

Even though casting decisions are conventionally the prerogative of the director, they are usually made in close consultation with the producer. On *Breaker Morant*, input was fairly equal between Bruce Beresford and Matt Carroll, although the idea to cast Edward Woodward as Harry Morant came from neither of them. One of their researchers just happened to attend a Woodward concert, and was struck by his remarkable resemblance to the real Morant.

'It was my idea to cast Jack Thompson in the film', Carroll recalled. 'Originally, John Hargreaves was going to do that role, and Jack was doing the Bryan Brown part. I think we delayed the production because there were still script problems, and, with the shooting dates changed, John became unavailable. So then we decided to cast Jack as Major Thomas, which he'd always wanted to do. Sometimes there are lucky accidents.'

'On *Goodbye Paradise*', said Jane Scott, 'Carl Schultz and I did the casting, with the odd appearance from Bob Ellis. The girl, Cathy, was very hard to find. There just weren't many beautiful young girls who were capable actresses. In fact, a hairdresser suggested Janet Scrivener to me, and at the same time the casting consultant, Michael Lynch had dug her up. She wasn't experienced — she was a model.'

As line producer, Jane was also involved in the casting process on *Crocodile Dundee*, although the decision making ultimately lay with Paul Hogan and producer John Cornell.

'In Australia, the casting was quite a simple affair. The characters were very clear-cut, and in the case of Wal, the part was written for John Meillon, so that was a *fait accompli*. Paul had strong ideas on a lot of the characters.

'Finding the actress to play Sue Charlton was very difficult. I went to Los Angeles a couple of times, and was also going to New York, setting up that part of the show. It was a long haul to find the girl, because we weren't quite sure where she was: whether she would be in New York — because she needed to be a New Yorker — or whether we would find her in Los Angeles. We retained somebody to help in Los Angeles, and also had somebody casting the parts in New York. Going through all the available girls was a long process. John would look at tape after tape after tape, and then meet a few. We taped Linda Kozlowski in Los Angeles, and brought her out here and introduced her to Paul, who was quite happy.'

'I won't take second-best', affirmed Buckley. 'I get into trouble as a producer, because I talk about the celluloid magic that some artists have, and some don't. That is what I believe a producer should be looking for. Certainly, let the director look for the actors, but that extra layer is elusive. There are some very fine Australian actors in our theatre, but put them on film, and they just don't have that magic.

'I have never reached an impasse on casting. I don't think any producer would force a director to use an actor, at least I hope not. Not unless the producer had taken the unwise course of casting the picture before employing the director. I can't see how directors can give their best if they haven't cast the picture.'

Similarly, all the key members of the crew are cast to form a cohesive collection of people who can work together effectively. Jane Scott;

'With *Crocodile* "One", when I talked with the director, Peter Faiman, about the crew, he had some ideas in his mind about who he wanted to work with, so we talked about the top-liners, and agreed totally about them. We agreed that Russell Boyd as DOP would be fabulous; Mark Turnbull as first assistant director would be terrific; and we talked about designers, and Grace Walker worked out very well.

'After that, it was a matter of discussing with each of those people who *they* wanted, and all the names started to get coloured in. One hopes and believes that if you have a head of department that you like, trust and respect, then it follows that you will like the people they pick, too. Now and again there may be people I'm not so keen on, which may be a matter of getting an assurance from the head of department that the person has changed, and it is all going to be okay.

'It worked out very well on *Crocodile* "One". It was a very good team. When we came to put together the team on *Crocodile Dundee II*, there were a number of people that we wanted straight away, and certain people I was keen we didn't get. John Cornell and I quickly sorted that out, and snatched up the people we were keen on who were available.

'The beauty of having experienced heads of departments is that they have so much to contribute. For instance, when you are discussing locations, everyone will bring their own expertise to bear. Sometimes it can be hard to talk a director out of using ghastly remote locations, which look good on screen. It is hard to deal with directors who really want to put their mark on the film industry with a beautiful film: the art-house film that they have been through film school to make. You can be standing there looking across a chasm, having come five miles along a winding path, and they say, "This is the shot I need. I'm not going to listen to anything else". You try every possible way to be positive about it, but ultimately you may have to find a better location somewhere else. It seems to be very negative to start talking about compromising the director's plans first up. But if you all know what you are talking about, and you have people who can contribute their know-how, then everyone is sure you are all trying to achieve the best possible result.

'I always go on location surveys. I did as a production manager, and I still do as a producer. The production manager, the producer, and all the other heads of department have to be around at all the early meetings and discussions, when you are planning money expenditure and the look of the thing. Pre-production is probably the most important time of all for me. You are eavesdropping on what people are saying, developing a working relationship with them, and making plans to spend money.'

The producer will also take an active interest in the aesthetic decision making throughout pre-production. If the overall concept of a film is being adhered to, this may be simply a matter of providing support and enthusiasm. The producer can also facilitate the exchange of ideas between department heads. (See in Chapter 6 Buckley's productions, *Caddie* and *The Irishman*.)

Once shooting is under way, the producer's degree of involvement on set can vary enormously. Jane Scott:

'If a production is really well organised, and everything is going fabulously, I *could* go off and have lunch with somebody, go to the flicks in the afternoon, go out to dinner, and then pop into rushes later. If everything is going fabulously well, my job lessens enormously. However, one must always be mindful of the problem that probably arises just as you were walking into the cinema, having skived off for the afternoon. Something awful could happen, and you wouldn't be around to handle it.

'One must also be mindful of what is going to happen to the film down the track. There is always plenty that one should be working on for later. As well as that, whenever there isn't that much happening in the office, then I would prefer to be on set, picking up on what is actually going on, and deciding whether I like what I see. While I like to be on set as much as I can, it is not that much. But I would be on set at some point of every day.

'During *Goodbye Paradise*, there was constant discussion with Carl Schultz, but at the same time I had a great deal of confidence in his ability. If he said "This will work", I'd be absolutely certain of it. He has some very good theories about what he can put across to the audience, and what the audience will believe. He also has a theory that quite often when a scene doesn't work, it isn't necessarily that scene, but rather the scene before.

'I wouldn't believe in sitting there and interrupting and commenting on set. You don't want to break the guy's concentration, but being there is all part of it, really, The best time for any input is during a block through, when the scene is still at its maleable stage. If you have a good relationship with the director — and this happened with both Carl and John Cornell — after it is blocked through, you have a chat about it. While the actors pop off to make-up, and the scene is being lit, you talk about how it worked, and whether there was a way of improving it. The relationship with the director should be interactive, trusting and positive.

'Obviously, if there are any changes to the script, and I'm there, it is something I would want to be involved with. The document that you go with has to be final. You shouldn't tinker with it while you are shooting it. The success during the production of *Crocodile* "One" was that we slavishly kept to that script. In fact, I used it to argue a couple of times with Faiman, and it was great to have that practically etched in bronze. It really was important.

'There was a scene in the script set in a car, to be done as a voice-over. We never planned to take the camera into the car. During the shoot in New York, it was suddenly discussed as a scene to actually be shot in the car, which I saw as a rather unnecessary thing to do. There are times when one has to suggest that things should be done differently; not necessarily from a creative point of view, but just from the practical point of view of getting something done.

'That film really was Paul's film. He and John worked very closely together. John was on set nearly every single day, from the start to the finish. He was there to talk with Paul, and to work out how

Paul would appear on screen. They are very close in the way they think and talk and work. So they left all the production organisation to me, but they both made the decisions which affected the look of the film.

'They knew what they wanted; they knew how they wanted Paul to appear. Until we actually started shooting, I didn't really appreciate just how clearly they saw that character. They knew at the outset that it would be very hard to find a director willing to work under that sort of close scrutiny and control, and it was often very tense.

'On *Crocodile Dundee II*, John Cornell needed support from the people he was working with, because he hadn't directed anything before. It was an extraordinary situation. A guy who had never directed a foot of film was directing a massive feature. Before he did it, I was quite anxious, really. But he listened very carefully to everybody's advice all the way through, and then followed whatever course he thought fit. He was well advised by Russell Boyd, Mark Turnbull and Larry Eastwood the production designer. He would seek people's opinions, and everybody gave him a lot. I was worried that he would let that confuse him, but he didn't. He was very good. He would listen to all that advice, but he's pragmatic. He didn't come to the film with a lot of highly idealistic views about how he would shoot it. He always believed that he would shoot a simple film about a straightforward story, and that the most important thing about it was the character of Crocodile Dundee. The audience is coming back to see him; he's the commodity. It was never in his mind to mess around with lingering shots of beautiful views. He was very easy to work it out with, and it was always quite a laugh when we talked about it: we weren't after filling an art-house. He was putting across a straightforward adventure story, and he was always very clear about that.'

Tony Buckley makes a visit to the set once a day.

'If I miss more than two days, I'll go and have lunch on set. I think you should take an interest in the crew, what the director is doing, and particularly your cast, because they all need a little bit of nurturing from time to time. But I think you watch one slate being taken, and then disappear. Anyway, you've got to be back at the office to make sure that your whole system is running for the next two weeks.'

Matt Carroll thought his main role during the shoot was to support the director:

'Unless it's a total catastrophe, and he's stopped shooting the script, you have to back him. The script is your greatest insurance policy. Providing he continues to shoot the script, and you have cast who you wanted to cast, then you must support him. It would be terrible treachery not to. Everything is on him at that moment: he's got the cast and he's got the script, so you've got to give him everything that you can give him to actually get it done.

'You can destroy a director. If you start saying, "I don't like that close-up. Why did you do that?", you can undermine his confidence so easily. It sounds simple, but you continually see idiot producers doing it. You must be supportive unless he really gets off the rails. If he suddenly starts going home at night and rewriting the script, then you're in big trouble. You've got to have a relationship with him where you can stop him doing that, and say "What's the problem? Why are you doing this? Why isn't this working?"

'You hope the relationship won't deteriorate to this point, but ultimately, if the director is not shooting the script, you fire him, and you've got to have the right to do so.'

'You must trust what they're doing', echoed Buckley. 'At rushes, you don't admonish anybody in public at all. I've been to too many screenings when I was an editor where I've heard producers do their nana.

'You detect at rushes if something is not right, or if there is something you want re-shot. We had to re-cast a girl for *Poor Man's Orange* in the first week of the shoot. She was all right in rehearsal. On the floor, the first day was terrific, the second day was impossible, and the third day we knew we had a disaster on our hands. The director rang me and told me it was hopeless. I told him to replace her, so he did. That's a producer's decision, to give the director support. If anybody's got a major problem, get there! Don't avoid it.'

With the completion of principal photography, there is once again more scope for input from the producer. Buckley's direct involvement in the cutting room is enhanced by his own extensive experience as an editor. By coming to the footage with a relatively fresh approach, he can more easily detect redundant or superfluous material.

'In *Caddie*,' he recalled, 'we did two nights' filming on Balmoral Beach. Caddie and her Greek lover were talking to each other about their pasts, which we thought was essential information in the script. We looked at the rushes and thought it was terrific. Then, when we saw the first cut of the film, I said, " What the hell's this doing here? I don't want to know any of this. Out! The whole lot, out! Seven minutes of it, out". It's never seen the light of day since, and you wonder why you didn't pick that up in the first place, it's easier to cut the page of the script than to cut the celluloid."

Matt Carroll is happy initially to leave matters in the hands of the director and editor.

'I always just walk away, and tell them to show it to me when they're ready. Then you've always got a valuable input, because you've been away from it. The director has been there every day of the shoot, and most of them can't stay away from the editing process, so they've got no perspective on it.

'For the producer, it's better never to see anything until the director actually screens something he wants you to see. Then you can make a very valuable input, because you're very fresh to it. Although you know the story from the script and the rushes, if you've got a good relationship with the director you can be immensely valuable to him. After that, you've probably got two more screenings, and then you're no better than he is. You're too close to it.'

Unfortunately, there is no opportunity for anyone involved to 'dry out', once this saturation point has been reached. Buckley:

'I would dearly love — and I think most producers would agree with me — to put the film on a shelf when you think you have got it right, and leave it there for six months. It makes a lot of sense when an innovator like Woody Allen budgets to re-shoot a third of the picture. But, of course, he is in a slightly different position. We certainly couldn't afford to do it in this country.'

Music is another area in which the producer may play a collaborative role. Usually, the composer does not begin work until the picture editing is completed, which Carroll finds totally absurd. Where the score plays a vital role in the total effect — as was the case with *Stormboy* — he likes to have the composer on board as early as the writing stage.

'It's creatively vital for the composer to be part of the process of the making of the film. It's a degradation of what the composer brings to a film to think that after there's a cut of the picture you can bring in this hired gun, and expect to get a good job.'

The final mix, in which all the necessary sounds are mixed together into one continuous soundtrack, represents some of the last opportunities for the producer to have a definite influence over

the aesthetic qualities of the film. This is also the point at which
the film really begins to come alive, with all the filmic elements
assembled together for the first time. So producers sometimes sit
in on the sound mix, which for a feature film takes about three
to five weeks (*see* Chapter 10).

After the final mix, many directors disappear, leaving the producer
to do all the remaining slog that culminates in the audience seeing
the picture in a cinema. He has to hound the laboratory to ensure
the print quality is exactly right, and, if the film is to be released
on video, attend the video gradings. There are posters to be designed,
and deals to tie up. For instance, if the film is based on a book,
the publishers may be keen to use the poster, or a photograph
from the film on the cover of the new edition of the book.

Without a pre-sale there is no guarantee that the product will
be distributed or exhibited. The relevant companies have to be
wooed by what they judge to be the picture's commercial potential.
These people can be just as fallible in assessing this as producers
can be when selecting scripts in the first place.

Stormboy had a pre-sale to Channel Seven, but no deals for the
cinema. 'When we showed it to the distributors', Matt Carroll
recalled wryly, 'they just looked at it as a kids' picture, said it
wouldn't take $100,000, and why didn't we distribute it ourselves?
We said, "Fine, we'll do that". So Peter Rose and I devised the
first ever schools campaign for a movie in Australia. We arranged
buses and study kits — the whole promotional campaign — and
distributed it in South Australia ourselves.'

This made Roadshow, a distribution company, sit up with a jolt
and take notice. It dawned on them that if they pursued this
campaign throughout the rest of the country, they would have a
hit on their hands.

'So we went back to Roadshow and said, "Look, that's how you
do it",' continued Carroll. '"I don't want to spend the next six months
on the road, organising schools and study kits. You're a film
distributor. Why don't you do it and make some money out of
it? We'll make some money out of it, and go on making films".
That's what they did, and it worked everywhere in Australia and
New Zealand on that basis.'

They are *still* making study kits for *Stormboy*. These have been
responsible for about ten percent of the gross earnings of a film
that recovered its production costs in Australia alone. And yet,
initially, no distributor would touch it.

With *Breaker Morant*, Carroll naturally expected the film to appeal to a predominantly older age group. This was born out by the scarcity of teenagers in the audience during the first weeks of its release.

'Then John Travolta and Olivia Newton-John went to see it one night in Melbourne, and there was a scuffle between a journalist and one of the bodyguards. Anyway, this made the front pages of all the newspapers, after which the teenagers just went bananas over it. The tenth week of release was its biggest week, just because it was reported around Australia that *they* went to see it. That's what really pushed it through the roof, because prior to that, it had just been the over-twenty-fives.'

Once distribution has been arranged, it might seem that the producer can do little more to ensure a film's success. Not so. Both Jane Scott and Tony Buckley learned this the hard way, with *Goodbye Paradise* and *Kitty and the Bagman* respectively.

'I had my belief that *Goodbye Paradise* would do very well in Australia', said Scott, 'and could become a cult film overseas. If I had been able to have a closer hand in the marketing of it everywhere, I believe it could have done those things. It is the producer who picks it up in the first place, and of course it makes absolute sense that it should be the producer who follows it through. The producer is the person who feels most passionate about it.

'The first release of the film was in Queensland, which it shouldn't have been, because of course the film is an attack on a lot of things up north. As the release hadn't worked so well, both Filmways, the distributor, and the New South Wales Film Corporation weren't keen to do anything else for it.

'In Melbourne I had no say in the theatre it went into. I went down there for the night it was to be released, and that afternoon I walked past the cinema, and there were no signs anywhere to say that the film was on that night. Nothing. I went into a phone-box and screamed about it, and by the time I walked back up the road, a guy was out putting the letters up, and they stuck up posters. About half way through the first screening, I stepped out to get some air, and they were taking the posters down! It was awful!

'I handled the Sydney release, and that did extremely well. It went straight into the Academy Twin in Paddington, and had a full house night after night. I had one of those faceless guys that you rent for a couple of hundred dollars to plaster the hoardings all round town with posters, and I had some good advice about using quotes from the film on those posters. I got some more money for the Sydney release, and spent it on doing that sort of thing, and some little radio commercials.

'The sadness at the end of all that was that the film got lost, and it shouldn't have. It was a very fine film, which at least was satisfying to have made.'

With *Kitty and the Bagman*, the exhibitors and the critics in the afternoon press all thought the film would take off. Tony Buckley even went to the expense of hiring trams to be carted up Pitt Street for the premiere.

'Then I went away for my holidays on the opening weekend, and literally no one went to the cinema. We couldn't blame anyone; the public just didn't want to see the film. Cinema ticket prices had just gone up to $7.50, and both *Ghandi* and *Tootsie* opened in exactly the same week as we did, which I think had a marginal effect. But, nonetheless, if they had really wanted to see the film, they would have gone to see it.

'Greater Union moved the film to morning screenings only. Then I found out that people were queueing, wanting to see the film at five o'clock, and it wasn't on. If I hadn't gone away on holiday, I could have insisted it be on at least twice a day, and I could have helped re-design the advertising campaign. You've got to work with the distributor and the exhibitor to make sure your film has a chance of working. So I learned a lesson from that: always be with a film when it opens; never be lulled into a false sense of security.'

After failing to secure a local distribution deal, Buckley had to act as distributor for *Bliss* himself, in conjunction with the New South Wales Film Corporation who had financed it. Every Monday morning he visited Greater Union, whose cinema he was using to screen the film. He looked at the attendance figures for the previous weekend and received advice on whether to spend more money on advertising. This careful nurturing of the picture paid off in enormous success for what was considered a totally uncommercial product.

From editing the script to overseeing the advertising campaign, with all that happens in between, an extraordinary range of skills is encompassed by a single job. This may in part be why it is often said within the industry that there are very few really good producers.

Producing is not for the faint-hearted. One might spend several years cradling a project — buying rights to a book, coaxing writers, chasing money — only to have it collapse like a house of cards when finance is unexpectedly withdrawn. And the producer is rarely paid during these preliminary stages.

Jane Scott has so far spent four years trying to launch a production called *Boys in the Island*, written by Christopher Koch and Tony Morphett.

'The hardest thing is having the conviction to carry on holding the flag for something through such a long time. One day you react to a script or a book, and say, "God, this is so good! I must make this". You build to a crescendo when you think it is going to go, and you are able to write fabulous synopses to pop in prospectuses and things. Then you start getting knock-backs and difficulties in different areas, and it's very hard to rev up the passion.

'All the time, one is developing other ideas, or carrying some other script. But every now and then they all collapse, which is one of the reasons I do a number of different jobs, (line producing and co-producing), apart from the fact I enjoy the varied nature of it. There is nothing like reading a script and getting on with somebody, and thinking, "This will be great", as I believed *Crocodile* "One" would be — and it was — and I was very excited when we started putting together the next one. It has been a terrific exercise, being able to produce something that you feel very confident about and being able to contribute creatively. I could open my mouth at any time, say what I thought, and they would listen. I don't think I could survive by just initiating films on my own. I need to work with other people as well.'

Whether the film is a runaway success or a dismal flop, it will require management for years after its release. There are matters such as other distribution deals, prints, subtitling and television releases to demand a producer's attention.

Considering that a strong, creative producer is a key ingredient in the success of a film, it is a shame that they have not received due recognition from critics and public alike. Tony Buckley, who has spent quite a lot of time lecturing in various film schools, had this to say:

'The sad and curious thing about going to these places is that everyone wants to be a director, or a cinematographer, or an editor. Very rarely do you find anyone wanting to be a producer. Yet the film is your baby: you have to put all those people together. To me, it's a most satisfying job.'

All three producers are intent on avoiding the staleness that can set in from continually using the same writers, directors, designers, and so on, or from making films of a similar style. Risks have to be taken to give new talent a shot, just as risks are taken on what audiences will like. As Buckley put it, 'Taking a punt with a ten million dollar film project on what audiences will want to see two years from now.' The risks are not just a gambler's lunge at making perfect pictures; they are necessary just to stay in business as the tastes of both audiences and filmmakers evolve.

But of course a producer only takes chances because of that 'passion' that Jane Scott spoke of earlier:

'In whatever capacity I am working, I have to believe in what I'm doing. I have to see something in it . Although my opinion may change as the production develops, I don't think I could go through the sweat and the grind without that.'

Remarkably, the producer may still have cause to sweat even when the film hits the screen. Tony Buckley:

'When the mini-series *Harp in the South* went to air, supposedly in stereo, I listened, and I listened, and I realised we weren't in stereo. I thought there was something wrong with my hi-fi. Where were all the effects on the soundtrack? They'd all gone. Disappeared. I had to ring the station at twenty to nine and tell master control to flick the switch over. That's when you know you're a producer.'

Production manager Antonia Barnard. *Photo by Jim Sheldon.*

3

Holding the Fort

THE PRODUCTION MANAGER

The role of production manager demands specialist managerial skills, including a thorough understanding of filmmaking, a gift for diplomacy, and an affinity with accountancy. The production manager is directly reponsible to the producer, and during pre-production works closely with the first assistant director.

Antonia Barnard's first job in the production office of a feature film was on *We of the Never Never*, set in the Northern Territory.

'There was so much to do, you didn't have time to think about it. You were learning on the job. We were in Mataranka, which is a hundred miles from Katherine, and over three hundred miles from Darwin, and they suddenly wanted a cherry picker [used to elevate the camera for very high-angle shots] in two days' time. I hadn't even the faintest idea what a cherry picker was. And where do you get one in the middle of the desert?'

Did she find one?

'Yep,' she said with a smile, 'from Darwin. The funny thing was, the driver never arrived back in Darwin with the cherry picker. They rang me two weeks later, and asked me if we were still using it. I told them we'd used it for one day, and then he'd left. He had a caravan attached to the back of it, and brought his wife and kid. He must have gone off camping, and taken the cherry picker with him!'

Almost every aspect of the making of a film relates to the production manager. Ultimately, the job is to bring the film in on budget. And yet, simply because there is a budget, the production manager must be flexible enough to bend the allocations of time and money as new priorities emerge during filming.

'You can never lock anything off in making a film', said Greg Ricketson. 'Different priorities will suddenly bubble to the surface, according to the way a project is developing, but you can create the environment where these sorts of on-the-run decisions are made in an atmosphere of quiet confidence rather than mad panic.'

In most cases the production manager comes onto the film at the commencement of pre-production. Sometimes, however, the producer will bring them in earlier to prepare the initial budget, or to re-draw the existing one. These budgeting decisions have far-reaching implications for the look of the film.

Ricketson was one of the first Australian production managers to insist on starting in advance of pre-production on a part-time basis. The film was *Puberty Blues*.

'The major decision that had to be made at the time of doing the budget was whether to shoot it in Cronulla, and around Wanda, as was called for in both the book and the script, or whether to just fudge it around Bondi Beach, or wherever. That would influence the way we were going to put it together. If we were going to shoot it in Cronulla, would we have everybody stay in Cronulla, or have people travel to and fro between Sydney and Cronulla, which was a big travel component for a very young cast?'

The involvement of the production manager extends to the decision whether to use a location, or to build a set for a given scene. While that sort of decision might be expected to emanate from the art department, or from the director, it will often become just as much a financial and scheduling decision relating to the way the production manager and the first assistant director manipulate the overall resources of the film. Greg Ricketson:

'I think a production manager should make suggestions about what the script demands, particularly when you are the only one who really has a grip on what the overall ramifications are. You can see, for instance, that a given crowd scene will use up ninety percent of your extras budget, and will take two days to shoot, while the dramatic content of the scene might be two minutes. That distortion of your resources means there are other scenes in the film which will have to stand back. Some scenes might have to do without any extras whatsoever, and other external scenes might have to be brought inside, in order to fit the budget. I find it very difficult to differentiate between creative decisions, and hard-nosed financial and scheduling decisions.'

Almost invariably the budget for actors is allocated well before the film has been cast. A particular role may be budgeted for an actor of median fame or wage level. When casting is in earnest, it might suddenly be suggested that the role by played by a Jack Thompson, a Judy Davis, or a Bryan Brown — that is, by one of the more highly paid members of the Australian acting fraternity — which may be of great advantage to the film if the actor in question consents. Such a casting decision would obviously necessitate either a revision in the priorities of the budget or a revision of the script itself.

The production manager is also the main hirer and firer of crew. Given the collaborative nature of the medium, hiring crew must be executed with considerable foresight and deft judgement of character. The producer and the director will appoint many of the key department heads, who, in turn, will suggest with whom they wish to work. As Antonia Barnard suggested, what emerges should be a team, rather than merely staff on the payroll.

Both Ricketson and Barnard prefer to be consulted on the appointment of department heads.

'I've always sought absolute consultation in crewing', said Rick-etson, 'and I've always attempted to put together a crew as carefully as you cast a film. My belief is that the mixture of people on the crew can make or break a film. If the chemistry doesn't work, the film is made in a negative atmosphere, and it shows on the screen. It can affect the way the actors actually perform.

'If you end up with, say, the director and the production designer getting into a squabble, then the designer may think, "Well, stuff it. Why bother dressing that particular area of the set, if it's probably never going to be used by the director". Then maybe the director would like to use it, but there's no set dressing there, so he restricts his shots, and it ends up as a different scene.

'On the positive side, if the crew is unified in really wanting a project to work, then there is a great level of excitement from working hard, and going off to see really terrific rushes. It's very gratifying, and when you get that atmosphere operating it's fantastic. Then, when everybody is under extreme pressure, you are far more likely to get a cooperative spirit.'

Maintaining that team spirit is just as difficult as establishing it in the first place. Diplomacy is constantly necessary as the limited money is doled out to the various departments and the long working days take their toll.

If all films were shot in perfect accordance with their schedules, the role of the production manager during the shoot would be reasonably straightforward. In reality, inclement weather, unavailable locations and sick actors are just some of the elements that conspire to keep them working even longer hours than the location crew.

Tales of catastrophe abound. One of Antonia Barnard's worst memories concerns the making of *Echoes of Paradise*, the story of which involved an Indonesian dancer. Director Phillip Noyce outlined the circumstances in which the film was made:

'It's very rare in the history of filmmaking that you are days off shooting a film that is predominantly written around one particular location — it is scripted, cast, sets have been built — and suddenly you haven't got anywhere in the whole world you can shoot it. It was just bad timing that we were about to start when someone wrote an offensive article in *The Sydney Morning Herald* [about Indonesia], and all Australian media were refused permission to enter Indonesia, let alone go in there and make a feature film.

'I was sitting in front of a map of Asia with Antonia Barnard, desperately trying to work out where, by next Monday, we could find a place to start shooting this film. We had the budget; the actors were paid for; the crew had started work; and the two lead actors had stop dates.'

'While the producer, Jane Scott, tried to have the Indonesians' decision reversed,' related Barnard, 'Phillip flew to Thailand to see if they could relocate it, and decided it was workable. But it wasn't possible to pretend the location was Indonesia, so the whole story had to be rewritten to be set in Thailand.

'The original writer wasn't available, so we had to get another writer in. And it was very difficult for the cast, who were already in rehearsal, to cope with what was happening to what had been a very fixed film.

'We were due to go to Bali first, and we turned the whole shoot around, and actually filmed in Sydney first. That meant the whole schedule had to be changed, and all the locations had to be found very quickly. The end of the story had to be changed a bit as well, so the writer was working on the script, which is a very difficult situation for the various departments, who are trying to sort out a location for the next day.'

The direct effect of all this for the production manager was an enormous increase in workload as hasty arrangements for transport, equipment, catering, and insurance were made simultaneously for both the earlier-than-expected Sydney shoot, and the brand new Thai location.

Peter James, cinematographer on *Echoes of Paradise*, was glowing in his tribute to the production manager faced with calamity:

'Antonia was fantastic. She and Jane Scott were a great combination: probably the best I've worked with. They made that picture.

'At lunchtime, Antonia would come out to the set and talk, and see if we were happy. She would take down notes of anything that might have to be done. The middle of the day is a great time to do that.'

One of Greg Ricketson's stories of catastrophe came from *The More Things Change*, when principal actor Barry Otto injured his foot on the second day of a seven week shoot.

'Barry was in about sixty to seventy percent of the scenes. In order to keep the project open, we came up with a variety of different alternatives, all of which had to be scheduled by the first assistant director.'

The first schedule was designed around the possibility that the foot would be diagnosed as a bad sprain, and Barry Otto would be able to continue in a week's time. Similarly, another schedule assumed he would be able to resume in two weeks. However at that point they ran out of material which could be shot on their current farmhouse location. Therefore, the whole production would have had to move to Melbourne for the two days' shooting that did not require Mr Otto. Even so, this scenario resulted in two empty days, with absolutely nothing to shoot.

'The third alternative was that Barry would actually end up with his leg in plaster', said Ricketson. 'There was a possibility that we would restart shooting with his leg in plaster, whether it be disguised, or shown as being in plaster, with a fairly major script rewrite as to his level of activity within the film. The particular importance of that one was that we wouldn't know until about three days later, with the results of the X-rays.'

As production manager, Ricketson had to concern himself with what impact each of these possible scenarios would have on the budget. The ramifications also ran to the size of the insurance claim for lost time: from around $60,000 through to a possible half a million.

'There was ultimately the possibility of just abandoning the whole project, which under a 10B(A) structure would have been an absolute nightmare, because of its effect on all the investors' tax write-offs. The real decision was whether to proceed, and on what basis to proceed, or whether to close the production down completely, and think about restarting it in eight weeks' time.

'Re-casting had to be argued very strongly by the producer [to the guarantors and insurance company] as not being a realistic option, given the number of actors in that age group. It had already taken about six months to cast, and there had been an extensive three-week workshop. A re-cast option would have involved closing down the production for a minimum of two weeks to determine who was going to be wheeled into the role, then put through that same workshop, as well as re-shooting that first couple of days.

'Our argument was that there would have been a very great difference in dramatic impact on the screen. And that was accepted very readily by the guarantors and the insurance company, which was interesting, because a lot of people would have said to close it down, recast it, and start shooting again next week.'

As it was, Barry Otto came back to them in two weeks, by which time they had totally run out of material to shoot without him, but had just been able to avoid laying off any crew.

Catastrophes aside, the day-to-day tasks of the production manager include hiring and returning equipment; keeping the set serviced with caterers, hiring extras; arranging transport for the artists; organising all travel requirements; looking at rushes; and ensuring the call sheet and the daily production report come out. The latter contains essential information about the day's filming and how the shoot is progressing, which is then distributed to the producers, the production accountants, and the completion guarantor.

And always there is money: for example, asking if a sixty-foot cherry picker would suffice in place of the requested one hundred and twenty footer.

Antonia Barnard told us how some members of a camera crew came back to her after the first week of a shoot, with several pieces of equipment they would not, after all, be needing. 'I was then able to go to the DOP and say, 'Look, we knocked back that lens you asked for in pre-production, but now the boys have sent this stuff back, so we can afford it for a couple of weeks. Do you want it?''

While most directors are budget conscious, they will almost invariably have desires that exceed the possibilities of the budget.

It falls upon the harried production manager to say 'no' from time to time. Ideally, one offers alternatives: if, for example, the number of action vehicles has to be increased, then perhaps the number of extras may be reduced.

Although the production manager is seldom kept on the payroll through post-production, his or her influence is keenly felt in the amount of money budgeted for this phase of the process. Given that these people often have little experience of post-production, this budget may sometimes be inaccurate.

On the rare occasions when the job does continue after the shoot, it is mainly a matter of organising and booking such facilities as editing rooms and dubbing theatres, as well as keeping track of money: how much overtime is being worked; what equipment is being hired; how much stock is being used, and so on.

By the time the finished product finally hits the screens, the production manager has probably completed another one or two projects. Unlike most of the key crew, their work is not readily visible in the finished film, except in the abstract sense: the very fact that the film was completed.

Greg Ricketson agreed that the evidence of their role in the film is more in the absence of negative aspects, rather than the existence of positive aspects. On *Careful He Might Hear You*, there was a very strong relationship between the director, Carl Schultz, the producer, Jill Robb, and Ricketson. With a carefully balanced crew on hand, he found it quite an extraordinary film to work on, because everything went like clockwork.

'Given that we were working with a very young child, from the word go I encouraged both Jill and Carl to rely on the fact that we would have to reshoot ten or fifteen percent of the film. We brought that into our schedule and budget planning from a very early time, and made some pretty hard decisions to restrict some areas in order to create that time.

'We ended up with six days of reshoots out of forty-eight, which were all absolutely necessary. An eight year old boy has his on times and his off times. And he had some very tricky emotional scenes.

'The rewarding aspect of that for me was just extraordinary. I know that Carl was delighted he had someone as production manager who was trying to give him time to work with this child. There are half a dozen scenes in that, which, whenever I look at the film again, I say, "Thank Christ we built into our planning the opportunity to reshoot sequences".'

The production manager's ultimate purpose is not just to be on time and on budget, but, like everyone involved in the project, to achieve both an absolute maximum of production value on screen, and a product which represents the original concept as closely as possible.

'The production manager's role can be one of the most critical and pivotal roles in film', said Ricketson. 'If it is done correctly, it should provide the environment for everybody to do their work in the most efficient manner.'

The assistant director team on the set of *Mad Max — Beyond Thunderdome*. First, Steve Andrews, Second, Chris Webb and Third, Murray Robertson. Webb and Robertson are in costume so that they can mingle with the crowd and direct extras whilst the camera is rolling. *Photo by Jim Sheldon, courtesy of Kennedy Miller Productions.*

4

Efficiency Expert

THE FIRST ASSISTANT DIRECTOR

To the casual observer on a film set, it may appear that the first assistant director does all the directing. Certainly the First seems to be ordering everyone around: telling the actors when they are required, telling the make-up and wardrobe personnel when they can have access to the performers, telling the extras what to do, telling the entire crew when to rehearse and when to 'roll', telling everyone when to keep quiet, and even telling the director when he or she is required. All this often involves a good deal of striding about and shouting, occasionally with the aid of a megaphone. The First is always there at the centre of the action, a mixture of orchestra conductor and traffic policeman.

The first assistant is hired primarily as an efficiency expert: someone who can ensure the job is done with a minimum of fuss, within a given amount of time. To the producer and production manager, a good First is an insurance policy, guaranteeing that shooting occurs as efficiently as possible. From the director's standpoint, a good First shoulders a great deal of the decision making, freeing the director to concentrate on more creative functions, and will also make certain that the director's wishes are conveyed to the necessary departments, and consequently that the director's 'vision' is realised.

The First's principal task is to schedule the film, and often a rough schedule is thrown together as soon as work begins on a new project, which sheds light on the feasibility of shooting the film within the producer's budget. If the film is budgeted as a ten week shoot, and the First is convinced it will take longer, then the possibilities of editing the script or extending the shoot may be explored.

The task of compiling the main schedule is not as straightforward as one might imagine. A strip of coloured cardboard is assigned to each individual scene, the colour being determined by whether the scene is interior or exterior, and whether it is scripted as day or night. Then, onto each strip is coded a mass of information, including the scene number, the length of the scene, all the characters who appear in that scene, extras required, special effects, stunts, and often a one line synopsis of the action. The strips are housed in a long concertina folder known as a stripboard. As films are never shot in the same sequence as they appear on the screen, the process of scheduling involves juggling these strips around into a shooting order that is both feasible and efficient. The average feature film has between 100 and 160 individual scenes to be accounted for, and a mini-series will have many times that number.

Normally, before shooting commences, all members of the cast and crew are issued with a fairly finalised schedule. By this stage, every scene has a reason for being shot on a particular day at a particular time.

The business of scheduling often seems like a Rubik's cube without a perfect solution. The mass of factors and variables affecting it include whether the cast are all available on a given day, whether the location is available, whether the set will be built on time, and whether to work the crew during the day or night — always ensuring the union requirement of a minimum ten hour turnaround between wrap on one day, and call on the next.

The order in which scenes are shot on a given day will in turn be affected by the quality and direction of the sunlight, the dramatic mood of the scenes, the deterioration of props and wardrobe, the time required for make-up, and the efficient use of costly items such as vehicles, livestock, and extras. Perhaps the most important product of the scheduling is that the First determines how much screen time, and therefore how many scenes, can be completed on each day.

Australian crews work a ten hour day, and it is imperative that each shooting day be exploited to the maximum, without incurring any overtime. Quite plainly, some scenes will take longer to shoot than others, and a large part of the First's skill is the ability to determine just what can and cannot be achieved in a day's work.

The *Bodyline* mini-series was scripted as ten one-hour episodes, but for financial reasons it was deemed more efficient not to shoot each episode separately. This gave the First, Steve Andrews, the daunting task of scheduling 888 scenes, spread across a nineteen week shoot. Beyond the usual factors affecting scheduling decisions, he had to allow for the varying speeds at which the four different directors (Carl Schultz, George Ogilvie, Denny Lawrence, and Lex Marinos) would work.

Even at the scheduling stage, Andrews believes it is important to consider an actor's state of mind:

'You make sure the schedule allows for the three-hour make-up job on the leading lady. You try as best you can to let her sleep in a bit, or schedule her scenes slightly later in the day, so she doesn't look like an old bag by the time you've finished.

'On *The Dismissal*, the ageing process on Bill Hunter, playing Rex Connors, and John Hargreaves, playing Jim Cairns, took an hour and a half each. That is a major consideration in your scheduling: to allow them time to feel comfortable, and to make sure they look the best they can.'

Budgetary considerations will also influence the schedule. Because principal cast cost less on a weekly, rather than daily basis, the First tries to condense the time span over which individuals are used. Likewise, if a hundred extras are required for two separate scenes, both scenes would be scheduled on the same day, where practical.

Weather is the wild card in the schedule. Generally, exteriors are scheduled before interiors or studio scenes. However, it may not always be this straightforward, as Colin Fletcher explained:

'Sometimes you find a script where there's just no work under cover at all. In those cases, you try and create wet weather cover. You might try and talk the director into doing an exterior scene somewhere near a verandah, so if it's raining on the day, you can shoot the scene on the verandah.

'It's a matter of being aware that you never know what the weather is going to do. You must always have some contingency up your sleeve, because ultimately, you are the person responsible for getting the film shot on time.'

During this pre-production period, the First is also involved in choosing locations. The First and the location manager present the director with a number of different possibilities for each location. The main concern of the First is the practicality of lighting, sound, and overall access. On location surveys for *Gallipoli,* for example, Mark Egerton looked at a perfect beach which unfortunately, was a five-hour trip from base:

'It was not really on. You should never show the director something like that in the first place. It's rather like giving a child an ice-cream, and then saying. "You can't eat it, because it's going to get your shirt dirty". However, if it's a major location that the director really likes, you'd explore the possibilities of using heli- copters to drop everyone in each day, or of building a tent city and living there for three weeks.'

Throughout pre-production, the First continually consults all key members of the crew, so he or she is aware of any specific problems or requirements they may have. The art director and the DOP are particularly important in this regard, but the list also includes the gaffer, the sound recordist, the location manager, the make-up artist, and the wardrobe department. If there are stunts or special effects involved, the First coordinates the specialist staff and other approp- riate members of the crew and cast to ensure that adequate safety measures are planned. There is a safety code regulated by the Australian Theatrical and Amusements Employees' Association, which must be adhered to.

When shooting commences, the First becomes something akin to a foreman on the floor. While the production manager runs the office and provides all necessary back-up for the crew, the First runs the set. This involves giving the director maximum support, keeping the film on schedule, ensuring the crew all work to maximum efficiency, keeping the working atmosphere as pleasant as possible, and keeping the lines of communication open.

Colin Fletcher finds this last point particularly important:

'Most problems in films arise from breakdowns in communication. It's up to you to make sure that every member of the crew knows what's going on. Then things will happen when they should.'

While filming is in progress, the First must constantly anticipate each step: the next set-up, the next scene, the next day's shooting. Eliminating hold-ups and hiccups requires a very organised, ana- lytical mind. It may seem that the First is doing everyone's thinking for them, but the fact is that he is the only person on set who is concerned with the functioning of the *entire* unit. Mark Egerton described it as 'a time and motion situation, where you can see that two or three things can go on, instead of just one thing. When you're ready to shoot, everybody's ready, rather than someone having to fiddle with hair, or whatever. It's man management, really.'

'You must understand what each department does,' said Steve Andrews, 'both on the floor and off the floor, so you can understand their needs. With the art department, you must be aware, for example, that the carpenters are working twenty-four hours a day to build you something you won't need in two days time after all. Or, conversely, that they're only working eight hour days, and you're going to need that 'something' tomorrow afternoon, so they're falling behind.'

As a switchboard for the lines of communication on the shoot, it is the First who knows when all the appropriate departments are ready, and calls for the camera and sound to roll, or 'turn over'. In a stunt scene, for safety reasons, the First will also call 'action' and 'cut'.

The responsibility for setting the mood on set falls largely on the First. This must be judged to a nicety: when to push the crew a little harder and when to lay off. A healthy supply of infectious enthusiasm obviously helps, which Colin Fletcher refers to as 'being a bit of a showman'. This on-set atmosphere inevitably influences the actors' performances.

'The actors should be presented to the director in a frame of mind which is conducive to their acting', Egerton asserted. 'Acting is an extraordinary profession; it is either "Hurry up!" or "Sit down and wait". We're working all day long, but they've suddenly got to come on the set and produce a whole lot of emotion at the drop of a hat. The actual running of the set when the actors are on the floor is extremely important. However rushed you are, the actors should feel that they've got all the time in the world to do what they have to do. The more you distract them from the job in hand, the longer it will take. If they're worried about getting their lines right because they've only got one go, they're sure to fluff it. Whereas, if they *think* they can have another go, they're liable to get their lines right.'

Steve Andrews was keen to reinforce this point:

'The actors are thinking things like, "Am I doing this right?" and "How do I look?". You have to make them feel comfortable — ask them if everything's okay. Just little things like that make such a difference. If you don't get on with the actors, then you're shooting unhappy people. They'll either hold you up and make life a misery for you, or the director won't get the performance he wants. After all, actors on the screen are what you're there for.'

It is the second assistant director who specifically looks after the actors and keeps them informed. The First chooses his Second and Third with care, 'If the Second is bad', Egerton said, 'and I find the actors are very agitated when they come on set, then the Second will go'.

Obviously the Second must have the kind of personality that is adept at dealing with people, including the occasional egocentric actor to be shepherded through make-up and wardrobe. Additionally, he or she is the First's liaison with the production office, and the production manager's major link with the set. The Second also draws up the call sheets for the following day, which receive approval from the First before distribution.

The Third looks after the creature comforts of the director and principal cast, acts as a 'gofer' for the First and Second, and helps govern the extras. As a general rule, the First directs all non-speaking cast aided by the Second and Third. Egerton prefers the director to remain divorced from the details of choreographing extras:

'Whether it's a battle sequence or a crowded airport, you're quicker at setting it up because you've done it before, and you know the short-cuts to take. You know basically what the extras have to do to make the shot work.

'You see films where the extras sure-as-hell look like extras. They've got no motivation; they're not doing anything except walking backwards and forwards. When the director wants people to cross in front of the camera, they really have to be directed so that they're doing something. If the director then fiddles with the background you've set up (it may be some little point he wants to see: a part of the background which is relevant to the main story, such as people making hand-grenades in *Gallipoli*), you really should have extracted that information earlier on, and also made sure that the art department knew about it. There's no point in saying, "We'll have the extras making grenades out of tins of nails", and then saying, "Well, where are the tins of nails?".'

Extras close to the camera will be directed and cued on a one-to-one basis, while those further into the distance will be orchestrated in groups. Part of the art of first assisting is to maximise the effectiveness of the extras.

'There is a principle', said Egerton, 'you can make thirty-five people look like sixty; sixty like one hundred and twenty; one hundred and twenty like three hundred; and three hundred look like a thousand. If you're good. Therefore, if the director says he wants a thousand extras for the beach scene, and you know that the budget, wardrobe, and props aren't going to stretch to that, you're going to have to start talking confidently that you could halve that figure, and still make it work.'

Steve Andrews suggested that 'The art is to watch the initial rehearsals with the principals. Watch the action, where the camera moves, where it points, what it's going to see, and how long it's going to stay on that shot before it pans to something else. The danger is that on "action", everyone runs from one side of the screen to the other and by the time you're half way through it, all the extras are standing on the side and the background is empty.'

Fletcher's most nightmarish experience with extras was having to make use of the general public in the film *The Coolangatta Gold*. The scene involved an 'Iron Man' race on a beach. A crowd of some two hundred thousand people had been attracted for a real-life 'Iron Man' event, and once this was under way the film version was to take place. With the enormous crowd and four helicopters hovering overhead, it was visually spectacular on a scale that no Australian budget could have created.

Unfortunately, the required number of shots were not completed on that day. They then had to try and recreate the scene, but with no budget for hiring extras. This involved not only having to attract people in sufficient numbers to the beach, but also having to keep them there.

'We hired a band, advertised on the local radio, and people came. To try and keep them there all day we raffled a motor-bike but didn't draw the raffle until the end of the day. We organised competitions where there'd be a cash prize of twenty dollars for long jumps, egg-and-spoon races and three-legged races. This was all to keep the kids on the beach so that when the camera was ready, the actors had been rehearsed, and we were ready to shoot, the crowds would cheer and do whatever you asked.

'This was hardly ideal because you never knew how many people you were going to have. They weren't bound to stay; they could just walk away. But they were fantastic. They were really tolerant. We were asking people to move somewhere else on the beach and all sorts of things, and they'd do it. Very seldom did we have anyone getting irate.

'Of course, I'd lost my second and third assistants because they were entertaining the crowds — trying to keep them there.'

Needless to say, Fletcher would be relunctant to use the public as substitutes for extras again.

Budgeting lies at the heart of many problems: it is all too common for the budget and the script to be mismatched. If there is a crisis during the shoot, the First's primary loyalty is to the director. If a film is falling behind schedule or the director has worked himself into a corner regarding coverage of a particular scene, a good First should be able to suggest solutions. But, as Egerton pointed out, it requires a canny sense of the right time to intervene without treading on the director's toes:

'When everything is going ahead, full on, you stay out of the way. If he's getting worried, then you can start suggesting things. That can still backfire if the feeling is that you're taking over. The thing is that as a First, you sit on the floor maybe nine months of the year. As director, you sit on the floor maybe ten weeks every year and a half. Now, for some reason, you expect a director to know what lenses to use, how to move the camera from A to B, how to cover a scene, and if he gets into a tight spot, how to get out of it. The crew, however, have seen people get into exactly the same corner before.'

In effect, the First must be as competent at the mechanics of directing as the director. There is certainly no point in making suggestions or offering solutions without being sure they are going to work. The ability to perceive an alternative is part of the First's role of assisting the director. New, or first-time directors are more likely to run into problems adhering to the schedule. Egerton has learned to overcome any frustration he may feel at working with a director who knows substantially less about the art than he does:

'You've got to give them exactly the same support you would anyone else. They might be the best thing since sliced bread, and just because they're only twenty-two, doesn't mean they won't be.'

From the director's point of view the First may at times seem like a sort of policeman. But the more experienced or reliable the director is, the less it will be necessary for the First to assume this unpleasant mantle. For Colin Fletcher, Carl Schultz is a good example.

'When I work for Carl, I haven't got to worry so much if we drop a scene. I know that he knows exactly what he's doing. He might decide he wants to spend four hours on a scene that we thought we would do in two hours. But I know that the next day he'll pick up the scene that we dropped. You can afford to give much more latitude and freedom to someone like that, whereas, with a director who has just started out, you really have got to be careful that the whole thing doesn't get out of hand. You have to guide them a lot more. If you are running over on a particular day, you've got to be really careful that if you drop a scene, you then pick it up the next day because the director is not going to be any better prepared the next day. So the whole thing can accumulate and finally you can be days behind at the end of the shoot. If the crew are inexperienced as well, you can find yourself really stretched, with not just the director asking for advice and help that normally you don't have to give, but the rest of the crew as well.'

The youth of the resurgent industry in Australia created an approach to the role of the first assistant which is unique in its high profile and realm of influence. The seventies saw an enormous lack of experienced production managers, so part of their role fell on the shoulders of the First, who at least had experience on the floor. To Egerton's mind this has created a cleaner delineation of roles than he has found to be the case while working in England and America:

'In England, either the production manager or the production supervisor does the schedule, and the First follows it through, which I find an absolute back-to-front operation. In America, the First is not a very upfront position. The studio system means that people are loath to be seen making a decision, for fear of being crucified for it.'

The extremely rapid growth of the local film scene during the early 1980s is probably responsible for the current shortage of good Firsts. During those boom years, promotion through the ranks came all too quickly. Many people were bumped up to being Firsts who lacked the vital depth of experience. At the other end of the spectrum, the most experienced Firsts may now have the luxury of being choosey about the projects they undertake. Colin Fletcher's job choices are made according to who the director is and the quality of the script.

For Mark Egerton, although the director is important when choosing a project, he must have his interest captured by 'some spark of excitement, some unknown quality. That's why you're not sitting in a television station and working for some studio. Also, I don't think directors necessarily need or want the same First. Of Peter Weir's six or seven films, I've only done three or four.

I certainly try and be available. I won't take a lesser job, like a mini-series, if Bruce Beresford or Gillian Armstrong or Peter Weir is coming up with something.

'Funnily enough, the end product isn't of great interest to me. Not really. I love the planning of it, and I love the making of it, but I don't go and see very many films. I don't find it particularly necessary for the job.'

On the other hand Steve Andrews sees as many films as he can squeeze into his busy lifestyle.

'My first experience of film was going with my mother, in our utility, thirty-eight miles into Dubbo to see Michelangelo Antonioni's *Blow-Up*. I thought, "This is fabulous! I want to do this". It was just this thing of "How do they do it?".'

Knowing how it is done Colin Fletcher finds that 'Often, the end product is disappointing. There's a certain joy in the actual execution of it: so much has ‛to happen in each particular scene, each particular shot. But sometimes when you see it on the screen, it's somehow not as exciting as it was when you were actually filming it.'

Scenic artist Billy Malcolm and production designer Grace Walker on the set of *Les Patterson Saves the World. Photo by Pierre Vinet, courtesy of Humpstead Productions Pty Ltd.*

5

Art for Film's Sake

THE PRODUCTION DESIGNER
and
THE ART DIRECTOR

'You never really design anything the way you want it to be, you design it around the things you can get hold of.' David Copping's maxim may raise the odd eyebrow, but most of his peers would acknowledge the underlying truth. The comparatively low budgets of many Australian features put a premium on the designing equivalent of bush carpentry. Knowing all the short cuts and cheap ways of doing things is often the only way to make the money stretch across the whole picture. With budgets normally locked in before any specifics of the look of a film are settled on, the designer's creativity must be exercised in simply doing the best with the funds available. This is worlds away from the designers of the golden years of Hollywood, which raises the interesting question of how the role has evolved to its current form in Australia. John Wingrove:

'In Hollywood in the thirties and forties, the production designer was a god; he was treated that way, he was paid that way, he was given credits that way. He was almost as important as the director, and far more important than the DOP. He was very much responsible for the entire look of the picture.

'That died out. My personal opinion is that it died out because people started making pictures on location, and, of course, sets became less important, so the designer became less important. DOPs became gods, because they were able to turn these locations into something beautiful.'

In the Australian industry of the seventies and eighties, the art department has responsibility for designing and building sets, approving and dressing locations, and providing action vehicles and props. The related areas of wardrobe and make-up generally have separate chiefs.

In the seventies, the art department head was commonly called the art director, and was aided by an assistant art director. In a prestige gaining move around 1980, the head of the art department became known as the production designer, and his or her assistant assumed the title of art director. Grace Walker, for instance, was fulfilling the same role on both *Summerfield* in 1977, when he was credited as art director, and *Crocodile Dundee* in 1985, when he was called production designer.

In the current context of the production designer being the boss, and the art director being the assistant, the degree of overlap between the two roles will vary with the individuals involved. Generally, the production designer is primarily concerned with conceiving sets, styles, and so on, while it is the art director who implements the concepts. The production designer may tend to have more contact with the director, while the art director sees more of the rest of his department: construction manager, scenic artists, props buyer, and so on.

Dividing up the art department budget and looking at locations are two of their earliest concerns. The producer has normally allowed a sum for the needs of the art department in the preliminary budgeting, well before any sketches or models exist. Even the breakdown of that sum into a specific budget, which is handled by either the production designer or the art director, is often completed before real discussions with the director have taken place. Wingrove:

'You think of how you're going to do it, and you budget for that. If it changes, then the budget should logically change, but it rarely does.

'I've done one film where the budget was totally insufficient. I knew it, and I still did it, which taught me one thing: never do it again! That's when it's way over the mark. Usually, you just haven't got quite enough. You've never got too much, it's always not quite enough. That part I don't mind. I quite enjoy that challenge. On *For Love Alone* we knew we could have done with another $500,000.

It becomes a matter of how we can cut corners, and still make a decent picture.'

David Copping affirmed this: 'Sometimes the adversity of having too little creates something better, because you have to utilise all the things you can think of. You can go on forever saying, "I need this, I need that, I need the other". Isn't it preferable to say "Oh, I've got this, now what can I do with it?".'

The ingenuity this attitude spawns came into play during the shooting of the mini-series *A Fortunate Life* when the money ran dry and Copping lost most of his crew. With a set depicting some huge buildings in Libya still to construct, limited time, and only four people to do the work, the solution had to lie in the choice of materials.

'We opted for $10,900 worth of one foot thick polystyrene, in bloody great blocks, four metres long. We put it together with spikes and glue, built to withstand the winds. Then the art director and myself attacked it with chain-saws. We built it in four and a half days, and then just threw buckets of paint at it.'

The choice of locations is obviously of huge importance to someone charged with the look of a film. While the location manager will do the initial hunting, the designer will generally inspect all the locations that make it through to a shortlist.

On *Crocodile Dundee*, Grace Walker went on the first run through Queensland looking for the right town. Prior to this, in the very first week when budget discussions were still grinding on, Walker had pounced on a pub which was being demolished in Sydney.

'We took all the stuff above the bar, and the bar itself. It only cost a hundred bucks or something. So the pub in the film had to look a bit like that.

'Then when we found McKinlay, I knew that was the town but I had to fight for it. You know, you *know* something's fantastic. It was what was called for; it was all there. Then I was dragged around all these other places that just weren't any good. I think they just thought there was probably something better. In a way, that's where I get a bit perplexed about them. You're employed as the designer to look after the overall design concept of the picture. So why do they argue? If they trust you enough to put you on, then that should be followed through. If I was a director I'd probably want to have the final say, too. But I'd still very much respect what the designer had to say.'

The selection and dressing of locations may seem like light work compared to designing and building sets, but in many cases, more effort has gone into this than the audience could ever guess. Take the hilariously climactic subway scene in *Crocodile Dundee*, for instance. The first question to confront Grace Walker was whether to build a set or find a location. The sheer size of a subway station was an initial discouragement to building a set. Then other factors intervened: if it was built in Australia, the crowd on the platform would lack the conspicuously New York flavour required, and building such a set in New York itself would have been prohibitively expensive. A location it had to be.

The next problem was finding a station with sufficient headroom for Paul Hogan to perform his 'walking over the sea of people' routine. This eliminated the functioning subway stations of Manhattan, and took the searchers into Brooklyn. Here they found a disused station to fit the bill, which needed little more from Walker's art department than a fresh set of signs.

For *Breaker Morant*, designer David Copping and producer Matt Carroll combed the South Australian countryside for a location resembling the South African veldt. Having found the right spot, Copping's only concern was whether they had sufficient money to convince the property owners to pull out all their fences...

The exchange of ideas between the director and the designer during pre-production will vary in degree from project to project, according to how much time there is and just how specific the director wants to be about the look of the picture. In an ideal world perhaps, designers would be able to luxuriate in a leisurely 'ideas' period between taking on a film and actually producing the goods. The reality is a constant rush, as is every aspect of filmmaking.

To illustrate the sweat of pre-production, John Wingrove related a marvellous tale of the making of *Mosquito Coast* on which he was art director and John Stoddart was production designer:

'We got the script on a Wednesday, were on a plane on the Friday, and arrived in Central America on the Monday, after a one night stopover in Miami. So we literally read the script on the plane.

'When we arrived at the airport they threw us in a car and took us to a building that was like Rick's cafe in *Casablanca*. "This is your art department", we were told. Back in the car, into town. "This is your hotel. Throw your clothes in your bedroom and come over here. We've got a production meeting".

'We were jet-lagged and tired; we'd read the script and that was all. They threw us into a production meeting with the producer and the associate producer. Absolutely zonked, we sat down at this table and the producer said to John Stoddart: [American accent] "Tell me John what is your concept for this film?". I thought, "Hello, we're in trouble".

'But it didn't turn out to be that way, in fact. They put us in our department and left us alone. The problem was we didn't have Peter Weir, the director, with us. He was in New York at the time, casting and doing other things. So we were unsure about what the concept was.

'In fact, we then sat down and in three weeks produced something like twenty-five different concepts. There were only three of us there: my assistant art director Brian Nickless, John and myself. So we worked very hard, and Peter Weir and Harrison Ford were to arrive to look at these concepts.

'We were quite surprised to find that, in fact, seventeen people arrived in the room to look at the concepts, which was a bit daunting. But they tended to be silent until the right person made the right noises. Harrison Ford was very highly regarded, his views were highly regarded, and he is a *big* star over there — we were amazed at how big.

'No one said a word. They had already had a Hollywood production designer on this picture, by the way, and he had been sent home. Harrison looked at this model of what Allie Fox would eventually produce in the jungle, and said "You guys have really done it. Now I *know* how to play this character".

'And, of course, seventeen people in the room said, "Yes, it's wonderful! It's fantastic! You're great guys, do a terrific job!". But until he actually spoke, no one said a word. We breathed a sigh of relief and we knew we were going to be accepted, I suppose.

'We were handed a full Hollywood construction crew, who were already there when we arrived, with nothing to do, waiting for the production design. So we didn't know quite how we'd be taken to, especially as the construction coordinator was quite a good friend of the designer who had been fired. But we seemed to please them. They liked the way we worked, and thought we were efficient; and they were amazed that at times Australian production designers will get in there and hammer something up on a wall. That was unheard of in America.'

Stoddart and Wingrove had the handicap of commencing work in the absence of the director. But sometimes even the presence of the director is of little use in the early design stages, particularly if the director does not have a definite look in mind. Basically, the overall design needs a launching pad and this may come from the designer, the director, the DOP, the producer, or be inherent in the script itself. It may frequently come from other films, or from the book that the screenplay was based on, or from photographs or paintings, as when DOP Peter James used the work of Ray Crooke for *The Irishman* (*see* Chapter 6).

Whatever the source of that launching pad, once it is provided, the ideas will flood in, accompanied by discussions and struggles to keep it all on the same track. Directors may frequently ask for more than is financially or practically possible, precipitating the inevitable paring down and compromising. Nonetheless, in the hands of a good designer and art director, it is amazing how much *is* possible.

'I find it very rare that we'll give up,' said Wingrove. 'We'll find a way'.

Some scenes may be discussed in considerable detail. Others are left almost entirely to the designer's discretion, which may mean pre-empting the way the director will block the actors' movements within the set. Wingrove:

'I have seen people design sets that seem to have no consideration for the director, or the DOP in particular. I think it's terribly important: where the windows are in relation to the action that's taking place; where the interior lights of the set might be. I certainly take all that into consideration and relate it to script pages and action. For a certain scene, I am imagining that the director will be in position A, that the actors will walk into a certain place within that room, and that light will fall onto them from a certain direction.

'It doesn't always happen that the director goes and puts his camera in that position, but strangely enough, it usually does.'

'I think through what I perceive to be the action,' affirmed Grace Walker. 'Obviously, if the director has another idea you talk about it over a sketch. But it always changes on the day, anyway. Of course, a designer sees in his own mind how the action should flow, but then he shouldn't jump up and down when it doesn't go that way. It's just nice to think of the best angles.'

Walker is used to having scene-by-scene discussions with the director but has found that these earlier pre-production discussions get lost in the rush as the shoot nears. When the DOP comes in on the pre-production, he may spark another set of changes, specifically in relation to lighting. However, if Walker's concept is actually jeopardised, he'll fight to save it in the face of DOPs who say it can't be lit and production managers who say it is too expensive.

One aspect of the process about which Walker was adamant that the designer understands better than anyone else, is the time factor: how long it takes to build a set, paint it and if necessary, move it elsewhere. This alone will sometimes curtail seemingly endless aesthetic discussions, so that the 'real' work may be commenced. Walker said he has even gone ahead and built things, while the director, DOP and producer were still arguing — and then presented them with a *fait accompli*. The three-dimensional reality has often delighted, where the sketch provoked nothing more than indecision.

These concepts may not be exclusively visual, as David Copping pointed out:

'I hear the sounds, I am involved in the acting; I am involved in the thing as a totality, feeling what the audience feels. If you put the wrong boat or the wrong car in a scene, the sound would be wrong against the dialogue that was going over it.

'In *Stormboy*, for instance, I wanted a boat that went tut-tut-tut-tut-tut-tut-tut-tut-tut-tut — because I'd heard it or seen it somewhere — breaking the silence of this wonderful place, the still waters of the Coorong, with the dear old man who believed he was right, and the son sitting in the front believing his dad was right, going out to catch a few fish to keep themselves alive. If you put the wrong motor on the back of the old tub, it would have been different. I was putting 1940 into a 1976 era, because that's how that man was living, and that's how that man had to appear.'

Design decisions emanate from a practical understanding of filmmaking as well as from creative impulses. On *Dead Calm*, Walker had to design sets representing boat interiors. These he built to a scale fifteen percent bigger than the boats he was copying, in order that the crew, the camera, and the movement of the actors could all be accommodated. Yet, on screen the size ends up looking right.

'I made one portion of it twenty-five percent bigger, and it looked too big, so we cut it down. It was something that we had to feel out. I also know what lenses do: that you can have a really big set, and think it's going to look enormous, and it never does. It never looks quite as big as you think it's going to look. So I thought that if that's the case, then I can get away with doing something bigger. I knew that the true size was not going to work for us. Besides, if we were going to build them like that, why didn't we shoot them on the boat, anyway?'

The designer's input can extend to suggesting possibilities for specific shots. On a location recce, the designer may point out to the director a particularly striking feature. Perhaps a set design inherently suggests some angles for shooting. It may be that the set is so stunning, or is such a strong aid to the story-telling, that it deserves more extensive coverage than was otherwise planned.

The opening sequence of *Breaker Morant* developed after director Bruce Beresford recognised the exciting possibilities of David Copping's unexpectedly ample setting. Copping:

'I thought it would be good if we spread our money a bit, to make the garrison look like it wasn't just carbines and smokeless powder that helped them to win. I scoured Adelaide for field guns and twenty-five pounders and we built the limbers, so that when you looked at the garrison in a wide shot, it showed that there was an artillery battery there, as well as just the horses and carbineers. It broadened the visual thing, and it also broadened the possibility of the audience coming to realise it wasn't just twelve Aussie horsemen chasing all these renegades.

'We made fifteen tents look like thirty. Outside the garrison we gave them cooking facilities that we'd seen in rough drawings: earth ovens, and using the black people that were there as cooks, and to serve up the food and clean dishes. Once you spread that sort of thing around for a director and you say, "This is all kosher, we've studied it", as he's walking around it, then he begins to see the thing in a much broader way, and he starts to use it.'

It all comes down to production value: maximising the on-screen value of each dollar that is spent. Copping explained how he pursued this goal in the mini-series, *Fields of Fire*:

'For me, the pub had to look up the main street, you're inside it so much. Otherwise it could have been so deadly dull, you could have done it in a box. Every time somebody orders a beer, the camera swings round, and the bloody train is coming down the main street! You're reminding the audience of exactly where they are, and it's production value. The train's out there anyway. Use it as much as you can. Broaden it. Open it up. Doing things in a box is easy. Then you get down to daytime TV. I'm not in daytime TV.'

Wendy Dickson is one of the few designers in this country who designs the wardrobe as well as the set. Normally a separate wardrobe designer is appointed. In consultation with both the director and the production designer, the wardrobe designer will develop a specific look or style for the costumes. Once the costumes have either been bought or made, they are looked over by the production designer to ensure that they are in keeping with the overall design concepts. For example, David Copping may have specific ideas on colour coordination between the two areas. In a heavily emotional scene he may prefer an actress to be dressed to blend with the set — 'be part of the furniture' — to let *her* bring out the drama, whereas in a preceding scene he may have elected to make her stand out as much as possible.

Grace Walker has a different approach:

'I don't really go into colours of walls in conjuction with what people wear. The way I look at it is that in real life you don't plan your wardrobe for what the colour of the walls will be. I hate seeing films that are what I call 'over-designed': when the wardrobe designer says, 'The walls are beige, so we'll have a beige frock'. And all those period films tend to look like that, which I think takes away from what a period thing is. I like it to be as natural as possible — looking real — except if it's a surreal sort of film, or whatever.

'On *Mad Max II*, I told the costume designer Norma Moriceau there was definitely to be no colour. We were only going to use black and bits of red. I'd hoped it could have been shot in black and white, and the director George Miller did too. Then it turned out they couldn't do it, because people don't go and see black and white movies.

'So then I said it had to be sepia right through. And in the end, it did have a dusty black look, very devoid of colour. With Norma, sure we collaborated, but you have so much trust in the woman, because she's so damned good.'

Make-up is another related area which involves the designer. However, compared to wardrobe the dialogue will be fairly minimal unless the make-up is special in some way, relating to the total design look, as in a period picture.

When discussion of a given design has resulted in some sort of consensus, the implementation of the sketches and plans begins. The degree to which the designer keeps tabs on items under construction will vary according to the complexities involved, and how busy he or she is. The wonderful cars that Grace Walker devised for *Mad Max II*, for instance, demanded greater supervision than normal.

'I kept an eye on everything that went on them. Every half a day I'd duck into the workshop and see how things were going. Or they'd come to me and say, "How the hell can we put this here?" "Oh, all right don't put it there. Twist it around here and do that". There'd be a lot of that sort of stuff.'

After a set has been built and painted, it still has to undergo a thorough treatment from the set dressers and props buyers. Under instruction from the designer, these people seek out the furniture, curtains, paintings, crockery, toasters, sherry bottles, *et al*, which bring a set to life; hopefully to the life of their fictional owner. This correlation between the characters and the rooms they live in may involve discussion with the actors themselves, the director, or both. Designing someone's bedroom means characterising them just as surely as acting that character does, and obviously the two interpretations must mesh. Actor Hugh Keays-Byrne has often supplied hand props that he felt were appropriate to the character he was playing. John Wingrove:

'On *For Love Alone*, he was trying to develop this character. He came to the art department early on with props of his own that he felt this character would have. If they'd been terrible we'd have told him to take them away. But as it happened, I thought they were extremely good, and we dotted the set with bits that he brought in, so then he could go to his own snuffbox, or whatever.'

David Copping said he provides his set dressers and props buyers with sketches, or, if they are people he has worked with before, he will refer to an item from a previous production.

'I let people go to quite a degree,' remarked Walker. 'I know that they're going to find something that I never would have thought of. A lot of the time the look of the sets is not just the designer, it's certainly the person who was props buyer/set dresser. When I was buying and dressing I liked a bit of freedom to be able to think, "That would be great there", because you're going round looking at all this stuff.

'I know well before the set's dressed, what's going in it, just from photographs, and everything that's coming back. But I will let a dresser have real freedom. I do that with everybody, and everyone feels better. It's more harmonious and it just comes together so much more easily. You know which direction it's going in all the time but you don't get pedantic with demanding just one thing. Otherwise someone spends a week looking for it, and you've lost a week when they could have been doing other stuff.'

The Stand-by Props is the person who assembles and checks all hand-props for the production. The Stand-by is also the designer's emissary on the floor, with a wide range of responsibilities, from ensuring undressed areas of the set are not exposed by unforeseen camera angles, to topping up glasses for a fresh take in a bar scene.

During the shoot itself, the production designer is often still working on design elements for forthcoming scenes which may be days or weeks into the future.

'The art director' said John Wingrove, 'probably has more of the day-to-day running checks to make; to see that what is happening three hours later is being prepared now; to see that the action vehicles have been ordered, etc. A day's shoot that might involve three locations means that you're hedge-hopping — always two hours ahead of the production, checking it's going to be there when they arrive. Then comes the worst part, of going back when they've gone, and sweeping up the mess.'

That the work of the art department does not go unappreciated is displayed in this enthusiastic endorsement of their efforts by cinematographer, Peter James:

'Art departments are always really pressed. I've never yet walked into an art department where they've been saying, "God, I've got all this money. I don't know what to do with it". They are always short of a buck — the poor relation in the film crew — and they are always short of people. They also work terrible hours: they are up well before everybody else to get things ready, and then they are still there, striking or preparing the next day, when the rest of the crew has gone to bed. They never seem to get their ten hour turnaround. I am very sympathetic to them. I think they are fantastic people.'

The presence of the designer or art director on set may give them the opportunity to press their ideas, but it also provides considerable scope for frustration. Wingrove again:

'Sure, art directors may try to influence people on set at times, when it's not going the way they thought it would. In a lot of cases, if you do actually stand and talk to a director or a DOP on the day about why you did something, they will go in your direction. They're not all cretins.'

The potential for wasted effort on the part of the art department is enormous. Most unfortunate of all is when a scene which incorporated an expensive set is cut out altogether at the editing stage. The tighter the script, the less likely this is to occur. A less demoralising form of waste is when a relatively small proportion of a given set ends up being seen. Grace Walker:

'As long as the bit that you do see works, that's fine with me. It's not my money that's being wasted. If you don't see it, you don't see it. It doesn't worry me. I hate this attitude of, "Oh, are you upset because we're not seeing your set?", just because you suggest an angle that you think is better. It's immediately thought that it's only to cover all this work you've done. It isn't. Out of anyone there on that whole set, who has thought about it the most? The person who designed it. But usually the DOP talks to the director, and that's how it's going to be done.'

'From day one of principal photography,' said Wingrove, 'you've really got to fight to get one inch of information either from the director, or to the director. That's one area I'd really like to see changed. I'd like to see some kind of avenue from the art department to the director, once you're rolling. Suddenly there are a lot more important things: the actors, the camera work, rushes, script rewrites, meetings with the producer... Changes, such as losing a location, often happen, but to actually discuss them in detail with the director is sometimes very difficult.'

There is a tendency within the local industry for production designers and wardrobe designers to be pigeon-holed according to the style of their previous work. John Wingrove:

'Everyone I know in the business gets very annoyed about it. People say, "I'd love to do that particular production. I know it's not what I've done before, but I'd like the new challenge". It's probably good for them to develop in that way. You can get stale.

'This used to happen when I was involved in stills photography in London. These people got more and more specialised. They would say, "He only does food. He doesn't do interiors or fashion." And then it got worse and worse as the years went on. They'd say, "He only does cabbages..."'

Australian art departments have reached what David Copping described as 'an assured professionalism'. He continued, 'Some of the most successful arguments for teamwork are within the film industry. You can design the biggest, best, most impressive thing for a film sequence, but if the cameraman hasn't lit it right, or the director hasn't got the people in front of the camera being convincing, then it's a waste of time.'

Director of photography Russell Boyd taking a light reading. *Photo by Jim Sheldon.*

6

The Director's Eyes

THE DIRECTOR OF PHOTOGRAPHY

The director of photography — or DOP, DP, cinematographer, lighting cameraman — has a crucial role in pre-production, the shoot, and post-production, which elevates the importance of his contribution to dizzy heights in the film heirarchy.

For the producer and director, the choice of DOP is one of the crucial early decisions. That DOP will accept or reject the offer primarily on the basis of who the director is, reflecting the closeness and interdependence of the two roles.

It is basically the size of a film's budget that determines the length of time a DOP is employed during pre-production. A common approach is to put in a week or so in the earliest stages, and then return for the last few weeks before shooting commences. The DOP can be just as central to the early discussions on the look of a picture as the production designer. Peter James:

'I think that everybody in charge of the look of the film — Wardrobe, Make-up, Hair, all the scenic people — should always get together and bring in references. We did this on *Caddie*, and it was a very successful couple of days of meeting. We sat around producer Tony Buckley's living-room floor, and everybody brought in references of what they liked: photographs, bits of fabric... Art director Owen Williams turned up with a packet of hundreds-and-thousands, and that was his reference for a party scene. It was perfect. So the wardrobe was like the colours of hundreds-and-thousands. Every scene and every page was done that way. That is the detail you have to go into.

'Some directors can't articulate their vision, but, because I have a very good reference library, once they start talking it will twig something, I'll be able to pull out some photographs and say, "Is this how you want it to look?" and the director will say whether he likes it or not. So that will become the reference, then, which we'll photocopy, and everybody will get a copy. That is very helpful in steering the look of the picture.

'I try and do that fairly early, because usually the art department is in already, and Wardrobe is about to start making stuff. I try and get in there at the same time, so we all start off on the same foot. It's no good the cameraman coming in later and saying, "I saw this whole thing looking like a fifteenth century tapestry", and the art department saying, 'Bit late now. It's all laminex!"

'In *Rebel*, Brian Thomson, who is a very strong designer, was determined to have a red look. The director wanted to go along with the designer, so everybody went with that.

'In the night scenes where the cops are chasing the protagonists, for instance, if I'd just lit it normally, it would have looked like it came from another picture. There was so much red in the sets, that I had to use red light. It is very stylised. It's not Sydney in the forties for real. To photograph all the red sets with white light would look pretty unsympathetic to the design. I try to give every film a different look. It's difficult, but *Rebel* certainly had it.

'*The Right Hand Man* had a definite look, also, which worked extremely well, though it was very hard to achieve. It was all like a tapestry. It is all in blues and greens, and is very dark, but not black, so all the backgrounds are just there — things like very dark oak panelling with little blue highlights in it. The designer, Neil Angwin, gave me some really good sets to work with.'

Tony Buckley, who produced *The Irishman*, described the extent of Peter James' contribution to the picture:

'After reading the script, he felt that the film should have a particular look. He presented us with prints of the Australian painter Ray Crooke, whose paintings have very dark interiors, but very bright exteriors, so you can see the landscape.

'The prints were purchased and given to every department head — art department, camera department, even the sound department and production office — so everyone knew what the film was meant to look like. Consequently, if you see a good print of *The Irishman,* the interiors were all set up so you knew what the action was, but also, there was always a doorway or a window through which you could see the entire landscape. It wasn't burnt out.

'It was a production design decision made by the cinematographer, but the art department agreed that was the way the film should look. That shows the input of each person on a picture. The cinematographer wasn't usurping the production designer's job at all — he was contributing to it, and suggesting a look for the film.'

Peter James himself expanded on this:

'I had met Ray Crooke, whom I admire very much. He lives up in North Queensland, and painted the Chillagoe area, and the Cape York Peninsula, which is where the film was set. I thought his affinity with both the landscape and the people he painted was just great. I thought it would be good if we could do this on film. I suppose imitation is flattery, but it ended up looking great.

'The characters were never alone: outside the window there was always the landscape, and it was so Australian. There would be a windmill, or a fence, or nothing — what you would call nothing, but you were still kept company by the landscape. The land was very reassuring. There's a classic look to it. It's fun doing things like that.

'I wanted *The Wild Duck* to look just like turning the pages of your great-grandfather's photo album, and it does. It has those brown edges to it, which together with the wallpaper patterns, the lighting, and the use of a device on the camera known as a lightflex, helped make it look as though it had been taken with an old camera.'

'Directors will talk about a mood and a look for a film', said Russell Boyd. 'Part of my role is to interpret that, and figure out a way of achieving it technically. On *Picnic at Hanging Rock,* Peter Weir and I talked about how unforgiving and unflattering hard light and lenses can be. So I decided to use the old trick of the gauze in front of the lens, with soft light, mainly from a window source wherever possible. It was the perfect picture to use that sort of look on.

'We had talked about the possibility of using diffusion, and tested different sorts: straight glass diffusion, fog filters, and the gauzes we ultimately finished up using. We did some brief tests the same day we did the make-up tests. Often you do filtering tests when you do make-up tests.

'The gauze look actually created a few hardships for me and my focus puller, in that we had to open the lens right up so that the cross-hatching of the gauze wouldn't photograph, which naturally limited the amount of focal depth of field. It was constantly a problem in bright sunlight. In fact, there are a couple of shots in the film where you can vaguely see the cross-hatching of the net, if you look closely enough. One is a shot looking up at Dominic Guard when he is in the boat with Karen Robson. I had to watch those sorts of things all the time, so it did create some testing moments.

'On *Crocodile Dundee*, director Peter Faiman, Paul Hogan, and producer John Cornell always wanted the picture to look big. Peter's brief to me was that he wanted it to be as spectacular as possible, and for there to be a definite contrast between the outback and New York. Well, for a starter, you don't have to work too hard to make them different, let's face it. One is blue sky, and the other is mirrored glass. But as a conscious decision I kept the outback exteriors, and even the Australian interiors, softer and lighter than the New York side of it, which I made a bit more contrasty and grittier.

'Both *Crocodile* "One" and "Two" are lit fairly realistically. There was no point in lighting any of the scenes overly dramatically. They are not the sort of pictures where lighting creates moods that are important to them, I don't think.

'On *Summer of Secrets*, director Jim Sharman practically insisted on shooting the entire picture with a 20 mm wide-angle lens, which is a fairly distorting lens, and not terribly kind to the likes of Kate Fitzpatrick when you poke it up their nose for a close-up. It was an experiment that was fairly risky, but Jim is a risk taker. Once again, a DP's role is to achieve what the director wants. A director can actually order a DP to use a certain look, whether or not the DP intuitively thinks it might be wrong.'

It is essential that the DOP has an opportunity in pre-production to look at all the locations which are being considered for filming. Russell Boyd again:

'On location surveys you are usually checking to see if you can physically make it work — whether you can actually light it and shoot it in the way that you want to — because of the restrictions of maybe a small interior, or not enough windows; whether you can make it look the way you want it, given a set of immovable parameters.

'The locations are usually well and truly chosen before a DP is called in, so often I have no choice. I *have* to make it work.

Where you have a longer pre-production period, you can actually have an influence on the choice of locations, which I consider to be a very pleasant luxury.'

'Some directors want the realism of being out there hanging off a cliff,' said Peter James. 'But generally they are inexperienced directors, because if you know the power of film, you can produce those illusions in cutting, with just one or two good shots of a stuntman stumbling and trying not to fall. Then you cut back to your actors, which can be done by a roadside cutting. But, if they want to shoot down the cliff, and they have the money to shoot down there, fine. Let's spend five days down there, which we could have done as half a day of shooting up on top.

'I've never rejected a location, but I have said that it will make it difficult to do. Given enough time and money, you can do anything. Nothing is impossible... some things are just very expensive.

'It is nice to be with a director on initial location scouting, because you are the director's eyes; you are the sounding-board for him or her to see whether an idea is going to fly, or whether an image is going to work. So you can go round with the director, who may say, "We're going to dolly here, crane here, then Steadicam down these stairs, and jump on this truck". And you may say, "My God! The audience is going to be sick at the end of that!" Or you may say, "Great! The film needs that sort of energy at that particular point". So it is very reassuring for the director to have the DOP there at that preliminary stage, to see how they react.'

The DOP will also point out advantageous or photogenic aspects of a location that perhaps no one else may notice. James:

'It may be something that wasn't thought of while the script was being written or while you were sitting in the office, but then you get out and move around, and develop an understanding of what the picture is going to look like by piecing together all these different locations. It's very mercurial.'

On *Echoes of Paradise*, the very late change in location from Bali to Thailand (*see also* Chapters 3 and 11) had massive ramifications for everybody involved, including Peter James:

'It was particularly difficult for everybody, because we went to Thailand not having seen any of the locations. But Judy Russell, the production designer, Clarissa Paterson, the wardrobe designer, and I all understood exactly what we were trying to achieve. We were thinking as one before we left Australia. We had already been shooting for a couple of weeks, so we had established a look. They had seen rushes, so they knew what type of lighting I was doing, and the mood that was being created.

'When we got to Thailand, and walked around these places for the first time, the decisions were made very quickly. Some things rejected themselves immediately, because they weren't of the look that we were after, and other things came forward that were the right look. It worked extremely well, actually. Phuket is a tropical paradise where you really couldn't go wrong. Almost anywhere you pointed the camera was fabulous: the ocean, the cliffs, the buildings and the fabrics are beautiful, and the people are lovely. That's what the story was about, so it wasn't as if we were trying to make it something else. As a location it was typecast.

'But we had already been to Bali, and had all our designs built around Bali, so it was a bit of a scare. The thing was to reject all the preconceived ideas that we had of Bali, and look at it as a new film. You had to keep yourself loose enough to take on anything that was going to come when you got to Thailand.'

When Merimbula was selected as the location for *High Tide*, Gillian Armstrong was keen for the seaside caravan park to look as bleak as possible, despite the fact that the shoot was in late spring. Russell Boyd:

'That story was actually intended for mid-winter. Gill wanted the caravan park to look as far removed from the festive season as possible. We consciously tried to keep the mood more dowdy — even the interiors. To a degree we had luck with the weather, but it was also the scheduling.

'We were fortunate enough to get big grey skies rather than big blue skies. There were even a few scenes where we would dearly have loved to have rain, but instead we had bright sun, blue skies, and the strong green of the edge of the hill dissecting the frame, which we didn't want.

'Even though the budget and the schedule were very tight, Mark Turnbull, the first assistant director, scheduled the film in such a way that on a lot of occasions we had two call sheets: one was for sunny weather and one for cloudy weather. There were what they called "A scenes", "B scenes" and "C scenes". For an A scene, it was critical that the weather should be dull and grey; for a B scene it was preferable; and for a C scene, it didn't matter. If it was sunny and we wanted dull weather, we'd either do an interior or one of the C scenes.

'That's an area where the director, the DP and the First actually can collaborate and help the look of the picture. The intention was to get *High Tide* to look like winter. In fact, I even printed it in such a way that it was slightly cooler, or slightly towards the blue end, so that it looked a little bit more bleak.

'I work very closely with the First. As a result of location surveys, I might request that the order of two scenes to be shot on the same day be reversed because, for instance, the one scheduled for the morning would be better with afternoon light. I also work closely with the First on the floor. Time is the big enemy of all DPs, and time is also the enemy of all Firsts.

'Likewise, I might go to the production manager and say, "The Louma crane came up in conversation on the survey, and it would be really nice to have it for three days." He or she might say, "As a matter of fact, it was budgeted for a week, so you've got it for a few more days if you can schedule something at the same time, and we can get it cheaply for the whole week." So then I might go back to the First and say, "There's another scene where I wouldn't have minded using the Louma. Can you slip that in then?" And all things being equal, that will happen.

'On the business side, a DP has to be economical, but our prime concern is to achieve what the director conceptualises. I have to work very closely with the production manager to make sure we don't slip up, or they don't undercut me, or that I don't go over the top in what I order. There has to be a balance between what they can afford, and what I can make do with.'

As Russell Boyd mentioned in relation to *Picnic at Hanging Rock*, tests are undertaken during pre-production to resolve many areas relating to the look of the film. These include lens, lighting, filter, hair, wardrobe, and probably most importantly, make-up tests. Both Boyd and James were adamant about the vital relationship between lighting and make-up. Peter James:

'You can totally change a face with make-up, and the face is basically what you are photographing most of the time. I work very closely with Make-up. Often, if you have a problem with an actor, you get Make-up to look through the camera. For a particular shot, one half of an actor's face may be made up quite differently to the other half.'

Once shooting begins, the DOP is primarily concerned with supervising the lighting. In conjunction with the gaffer, he works out the selection and placement of lights, their angles and intensities. It may appear, therefore, that their main work is lighting interiors, but this is a misconception that Boyd was keen to dispel.

'Exterior lighting is more demanding in that you have less control. You might start a scene with not a cloud in the sky, but by lunchtime it has clouded over, and you have to match the light.

'Also, film emulsion does not handle contrast the way your own eyes do, so you have to fill out or light up shadow areas. Otherwise the film is too contrasty and there is too little detail in the dark areas. You have to throw light in there so the detail will register on the film emulsion. By the dark areas, I basically mean the shadow side of faces. If an actor is wearing a hat which is throwing shadow all over his face, you naturally have to light up that shadow area, so it will read with an acceptable amount of detail.

'Quite often while I'm lighting a scene, I will have second thoughts about whether I'm on the right track, and just check with the director that what I'm doing is within the parameter of the way they feel, as well. I might say, "I'm putting this guy in a bit of shadow here. Is that alright?" The director may tell me the actor has a line of dialogue that is fairly important, so I may suggest he be moved a bit closer to the window. Or the director might say, "Yeah, make it as dark as you like, because it's sinister".

'Usually, the emotional content of a scene is pretty well determined by discussion in pre-production, and what the script might suggest. A director may come up to you at rushes and say, "I thought it was going to be a bit more low key than that", or whatever, but you are usually working with a success rate of ninety-nine percent, I suppose.

'A DP's role is very supervisory in the areas of both lighting and camera. I will always keep an eye on what is happening with the camera, so if there are any changes, I'll know about them — or maybe make my own suggestions as to other changes. I may think, "Perhaps we should do a little track-shot there, instead", which will save a set-up, or might enhance getting the actors into position for a close-up, or whatever. If the director and the operator are going well together, I'll just keep an ear open for any changes to the framing.

'Some directors will come to you and say, "We want to start with the camera here; actors will walk into shot; one of them will speak, we want to track with them, going close during the track, pull back", and so on. They'll explain the whole shot, and you mechanically set it up and light it, and the operator will set up the camera on the dolly. In those sorts of instances, the DP and the operator have very little to do with the choreography of the action of the camera and the actors.

'With directors who are more performance orientated or story orientated — not quite as visual — a DP can be quite a force in the overall picture.'

More than anyone else on set, the DOP is likely to contribute to the director's ideas on how to cover a scene. Peter James:

'I like to work with someone who knows how the film is going to cut together. But it is nice to be listened to when you have an opinion on what you think is a better angle. Whether it is better or not is really the director's decision to make. If they reject it, that's fine. It doesn't stop you from coming up with the suggestions. I think if they take one idea in ten, it's probably a pretty good average. If a director takes every idea you come up with, you worry about the director, because maybe you should be directing the show and not that director! If a director took every idea that anybody suggested, the show would be an absolute nightmare. Really, all you want is to be the devil's advocate, and they can think about your suggestion, and accept it or reject it. It doesn't hurt my ego if it's turned down.

'It's an area where, as an experienced director of photography, it is easy to overwhelm a young director, because it might be their first time on a big feature set, and it can be a bit disorienting for them. Sometimes they can rely on you too much. You are there to reassure them, but not to do it for them.

'On the other hand, there are directors who know exactly what lenses they are going to use, and exactly where they are going to put the camera. It is all plotted. That is probably a little too organised for me, in that it doesn't leave anything to chance. It doesn't leave any room for the "X" factor to happen. An actor might be feeling terrific and giving a great performance; therefore we really should cover a separate close-up or side angle, which is not really necessary, but might be a wonderful thing to have in the editing room. Just to go to that angle once could make the scene.'

'Working with a director who hasn't done a lot of preparation,' added Boyd, 'but who is ready for advice, and in fact solicits help in the choreography of a scene, or the choreography of the camera, is a totally rewarding part of a DP's job; you can actually feel like you are making a contribution to the overall fluidity of the film.'

'It is only natural,' opined James, 'that it is the DOP who is the main source of a second opinion for the director. As a cameraman,

I always try and be the audience. It's tough sometimes, when it is snowing or raining, or it is night with dawn coming up, and you still haven't got the shots. But despite incredible physical inconvenience, you must try and think clearly as to where you would like to be viewing this film from, to put the audience in the best seat in the house.'

Coping with 'physical inconvenience', particularly lighting problems at the beginning and end of a day, are a fact of life. Russell Boyd recalled the making of the scene in *Gallipoli* when Mark Lee and Mel Gibson are on the pyramid:

'It was a dawn scene. We had to stagger up the pyramid — one of the smaller ones, thank God — with all our equipment, and get the whole scene set up and rehearsed before the first rays of sunshine spread across the horizon. Invariably in that sort of situation, you are caught fifteen minutes short, whatever you do, because you can't stop the old sun, even in Egypt. It's been striking those pyramids for quite a while.

'It was complete panic to get everything right. We were changing filters left, right and centre, and Peter Weir was getting his actors to perform correctly. It's one of those times where you are really flying by the seat of your pants, trusting your experience, and you probably don't sleep until you see rushes the next night. But hopefully you make as few mistakes as possible, and cut the takes up so that the audience will never know about the panic.

'Usually, the panic occurs at the end of the day, when you are pushing to match the light that you've had all through the day. Invariably, you'll have three or four shots to go, and it becomes a collaboration between the director, DOP, and First, as to how to make the three shots the director wanted work in one shot, to save time in setting up, moving the camera, and marshalling all the troops. Quite often you cannot come back to the same location the next day, because you are off to somewhere else.

'Peter Weir once said that the greatest filmmakers are the ones who learn the art of compromise, and I think that is quite true. It's not only at the end of the day, but right through the picture. To be able to turn a compromise into a plus is quite an art. I think that's where you'll find the survivors in the film industry.'

Boyd described shooting the opening of *High Tide*, in which the camera travels rapidly and very smoothly over some seaside rock formations.

'That was a shot that Gill specifically wanted, which was a bit of a challenge. We didn't really have the money for Steadicam, and anyway, I would have preferred to use the money elsewhere, in terms of equipment. So she got me thinking about how to achieve it, and I came up with the simplest solution I could, which actually worked effectively. We mounted the camera directly on to a flat aluminium plate, which had a handle out each side. My camera-assistant, Andy McLean and I just hand-held it as we ran over the rocks. We were able to actually keep it quite low to the ground, and as we saw a rock, we'd just lift over the top of it.

'But I kept photographing my foot all the time. At rushes the next night, in nearly every take my sneaker came into shot, pounding away over the rocks. But there were enough okay takes: we shot it over a couple of days.'

If every problem could be swung to a film's advantage, flawless motion pictures would be the norm. When we asked Boyd if there were any shots in his projects that subsequent viewing makes him long to re-do, his response was, 'How long have you got?' However, most of these mistakes are only apparent to the filmmaker, who knows the attendant circumstances. The audience is generally none the wiser. Boyd:

'There was a scene in *Crocodile Dundee* which we re-shot about four times, and it was never really right. It was very early in the film, where Paul Hogan and Linda Kozlowski are driving through the outback in the safari vehicle — the big International with the boat on top and the covered wagon thing — that Grace Walker designed so well.

'First, we tried doing it from a tracking vehicle; second, we tried it from bonnet mounts; third, we tried it hand-held; and fourth, we did it hand-held again, because the damn thing was so bumpy.

'We shot it on a road, going from east to west in the morning, and west to east in the afternoon, so it would always be back lit. But I kept being fooled by the direction of the road, which would curve around, and suddenly there would be hard front light all over Linda's face. It was just a nightmare. Whenever I see *Crocodile* "One", that scene always sends a shiver up my spine.'

Peter James is of the opinion that many problems encountered on location could be circumvented by using studio sets instead.

'Most directors in Australia are from documentary backgrounds, so they are conditioned to think, "I'll go on location and do it". On *The Wild Duck* we had a studio set of this house, which I lit while the art department was still finishing it off. I could see I

87

was going to get into trouble with doorways and columns and things like that. There was a small hallway with a door at the top of a couple of stairs, which was very hard to light, so the painter just painted all my shadows in for me. I lit it the best way I could, to get the most even exposure on the area that I needed, and then he painted all the shadows in with a spray-gun.

'It was fantastic. That's another way in which you work with people. He had a ball, because he could see what was happening now that it was lit. Normally, they just work with a work light. The painters are just gold to me.'

Within the camera department, the DOP heads a team that includes the clapper/loader, focus puller, and camera operator (*see* Crew Roles). For reasons of time and established work practice, it is more frequent for an operator to work the camera than for the DOPs to do it themselves. Time may be saved by the operator and director working on the camera placement and shot composition, while the DOP is busy lighting. Russell Boyd:

'Operating is one of film's greatest jobs, and can be very rewarding in terms of the contribution made. An operator can help tell a story very much on the same level as the director or DP. He or she can have an enormous influence on the story through camera angles, composition, and camera movement.

'I always want to be involved in it, and my charter is to supervise it. It depends on the way the director wants to work. Some like working with an operator, and almost exclude the DP. Others like working through the DP, who then transmits the ideas to the operator.

'I generally work with operators for half a dozen pictures before they move on. We always talk about composition before a picture starts. During the picture I look through the camera in ninety-nine percent of the set-ups. I chat to the operator about composing a bit to the right or left, or with more sky or less sky. But generally, apart from their own experience, they know what I want as well, so a lot goes unsaid.'

On 16 mm telemovies, where the camera equipment is smaller, lighter, and more portable, Boyd usually does his own operating. He also operated on *High Tide*.

'Gill presented *High Tide* to me as a smaller, more ensemble sort of film. I suggested I operate, and she jumped at the idea, because I think she felt that the camera would be slightly more single-minded: there wouldn't be two people putting in their ten cents' worth.

'It is the camera operator's role to make suggestions to the director. Often a DP will get together with the director and the operator at the beginning of a set-up, and then he'll be off lighting. The director can then work with the operator to fine-tune the camera angle. But I collaborate very closely with operators when I have them, which is most of the time, and I appreciate the help they can be to me. I don't mind working either way. It's much harder, physically and mentally, without an operator, but you do feel a bit more satisfied.'

'I've only used two operators', said Peter James, 'Johnny Seale and Danny Batterham [both now DOPs]. With people of such skill, I find it's a whole area of the picture I can almost leave to them; just let them do their thing with the director. That is not to say that I'm not interested in how the camera moves. But I find it is such a big area, it is better to put the responsibility on to them. It's really a separate area. I'm involved in the overall look of the picture, with the director, and I'm really busy lighting. I enjoy operating, but I think it's unfair on the actors and the director, because you hold up the set. While you are lighting, you can't be operating, and vice versa. So either the electrician is waiting for you to get off the dolly, or the actors and director are waiting for your opinion on how a rehearsal is looking. I find it easier to be outside the camera, and with a good operator I know exactly what they are getting. I look through the camera occasionally, mainly for lighting. I have implicit faith in the operator. If I didn't, I wouldn't have them: I'd do it myself.

'The director often talks more to the operator than to me. Sometimes I don't need to talk to the director, because we've basically said everything that is necessary.'

Finally, after the film has been shot, edited, and the soundtrack has been mixed, the negative is matched to the work print, and it is time to run off a complete print in the laboratory. Here the DOP is called back in to supervise the grading process. Grading is essentially a matter of making the colour tones and light intensity consistent throughout a film because shots may vary due to different filters, lenses, exposures, batches of film stock and conditions. Dialogue between the DOP and the grader is established as early as pre-production, when the make-up tests are printed, and continues throughout the shoot as the laboratory processes each day's rushes. Without personal contact, the results can be disastrous. Peter James:

'I did a film years ago, which went to America to be graded. The grader eventually had to send us a clip of the film, and told us he was having terrible problems because he had red ground, blue sky, pink clouds, and white trees. We'd been shooting in the outback, where you do have those colours. He was trying to make the red ground green, and everything was turning out the wrong colour.

'Often you find the Panavision zoom lenses are much more yellow than the standard Panavision lenses, so the material shot on the standard lens needs a lot more yellow added to it to match up to the zoom lens, to balance out the colour.

'You may have exposed your night scenes lighter than you want them so you can bring them down three or four printer lights, to make the blacks richer. You may find that coming out of a night scene into a bright sunny day is just too much of a shock, or it may be just the shock you want. You may want that first shot to be a little bit brighter than the next couple of shots, so that the audience's eyes hurt when you come from the night into the day. There might be a music sting to go with that — a big bang or something. So you do all that in the grading.'

The whole process only takes a couple of days, but frequently the DOP is at work on a new project by that time, and his presence may be sorely missed. Russell Boyd, for example, was unavailable for the final grading of *Mrs Soffel*. In fact, *Mrs Soffel* makes an interesting case study in the way that grading is the final step in realising a given look that was defined way back in pre-production. Boyd:

'*Mrs Soffel* was set in Pittsburg at the turn of the century, at the height of the black and polluted skies. It was an industrial wasteland, virtually. I agreed with Gill's strong ideas about keeping it dark and dirty. Often I'd shoot a scene which we'd see at rushes the next evening, and Gill would say I hadn't gone far enough, and I'd say, "But we can always print it down".

'In retrospect, maybe I went too far, for which I copped a lot of criticism from the press. One of them — I think it was the critic for the *New York Times* — said, "Didn't Mr Boyd realise there was electric light in those days?" I have seen plenty of movies that are darker than that, and have gotten away with it. But it did cause me to re-examine how far I should go in terms of under-exposure, and how far I can stretch the latitude of the film emulsion.

'Some of the prints were *extremely* dark. That was a problem of not being able to be present for the grading of the film. There may have been a minor communication problem on a technical level, because I wasn't there. In fact, Gill spoke to the grader, and told him we wanted it dark and dirty and dingy, the way we had shot it. He actually made what I consider was a very nice print, but boy was it dark. I was a little concerned that it might have been too dark, but, as I said. I've seen lots of pictures that were darker all the way through.

'As is often the case, they made six of the initial release prints to go round the country for previews, and that very dark print was the one the critics saw. Once they started complaining about how dark it was, we immediately made the rest of the prints a few points lighter.

'Whether the critics were right or wrong is open to conjecture, really. It's all subjective. I'm not saying it was a work of art and they didn't realise it, but that was the way I saw the picture, and I still see it that way. I might light it slightly differently now, having borne the criticism. Maybe I wouldn't.'

From the initial talks in pre-production, right through to the final grading, there ideally runs that golden thread of a homogeneous vision: from Gill Armstrong saying at the outset of *High Tide* that she envisaged it as being set in winter, through to Russell Boyd ensuring the grading leant towards the blue end of the colour spectrum.

'The thing is to have that dream,' asserted Peter James, 'to have that vision of how you are going to transport that script. Maybe people come to me for that input: not just to take pictures but to take a film visually somewhere they hadn't thought about. But it's not only the look that the cinematographer can give your film; it's *themselves* as a sounding-board; *their* opinions; *their* personality. And I think that goes for all crew members.'

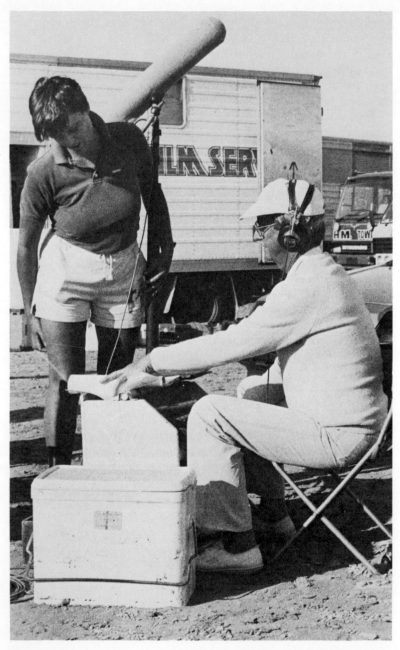

Boom swinger Sue Kerr and sound recordist Syd Butterworth. *Photo by Tony Wellington*

7

All Ears

THE SOUND RECORDIST

'**G**enerally, by asking a director what style of sound they want, you are suddenly confronting him or her with a realisation that they haven't thought about it up to that point', observed Mark Lewis. 'In pre-production they are very aware of, say, telling the art department what they want the film to look like — whether it's going to be all red, or period, or stylised; they're aware of what the make-up and wardrobe departments are doing, and they start developing a camera style. But I don't think the majority of directors in Australia are very aware of the potential of sound as a stylistic element in making their films.'

Both Lewis and Syd Butterworth have found it useful to initiate some discussion with the director prior to the shoot. Butterworth:

'It's a good idea to have as much information as possible in advance from the director: how they're going to cover certain scenes, or what the general feeling throughout the film will be. There could be words said on that score, but they have to leave it to you to decide how to do it. You get a general idea of what a film is to be like, and then you largely use your own initiative. They tend to leave it to you on the day.'

The sound recordist joins the sizeable number of people who look at potential locations during pre-production. More often than not the locations have already been selected for their visual merits, so the recordist's job is simply to make the best of it. He or she decides if sound-proofing or sound treatment of any kind is required and notifies the production office if the sound quality will be so bad as to necessitate post-syncing. A willingness to compromise is often mandatory: if a scene is set on the Sydney Harbour Bridge, one can hardly complain that it is too noisy... Syd Butterworth:

'I've worked in the most extraordinary places, such as a factory in Botany which is within a few hundred yards of one of the runways at Mascot airport. We did *Les Patterson Saves the World* there, which had huge sets, so they had to have somewhere big.'

If the sound recordist knows in pre-production about potential complications, such as lines that must be whispered on a very noisy location, there is time to plan a solution.

'In *For Love Alone*', Syd recalled, 'we used a boat shed with water lapping underneath it, a mill creaking away in the background, and even rain on the roof at one stage. Everything was against this intimate scene of two people with quiet things to say to one another. Obviously the director required the artists to speak very quietly, so in the interests of retaining the location sound I used a radio mike, which I would normally try to avoid using.'

Butterworth thinks the unique ambience captured on location makes a much greater contribution to a picture than is commonly acknowledged, and this is why location sound is generally preferred to radio mikes or post-sync sound.

'I feel it is important to capture the movements of the artists and the sound of a room. Whether they're turning as they speak, or looking out a window and talking, the sound changes very subtly. Whereas, if it's post-sync, you very seldom get the feeling of someone actually doing something in a room.' An attempt to re-create acoustic variations in post-sync can result in subtle, possibly subliminal distractions for the audience.

The economics of location versus post-sync must be considered also. If $300 in sound-proofing will render a location useable, then $800 might be saved in post-syncing. The 'cleaner' a location is soundwise, the better — a fact which the sound recordist will impress on the location manager and first assistant.

Pre-production is also the time for the recordist to let the production office know what special equipment he is going to need, and to scan the script for ideas that may contribute to the success of the film.

'Sometimes those ideas are accepted and sometimes they are rejected', Lewis said. 'At other times, you might have all the great ideas in the world but when it comes to shooting on the day, it's such a bun-fight you don't have time to do even a one minute atmosphere track.'

In some cases, unless sound is thought about in pre-production, opportunities for building atmosphere into the film may be lost. For instance, a scene set in a lush jungle with a soundtrack saturated with exotic bird calls and so on, may sound so exaggeratedly rich as to seem false, despite being an *audio verité* recording. Mark Lewis:

'If a character is given a line like, "This jungle gives me the creeps", it cues the audience's reactions to the soundtrack, making it believable. It's a matter of incorporating the soundtrack with the image.'

A good example of this relationship occurred in *Silver City*, a film about migrants arriving in Australia. Mark takes up the story:

'During the course of the film, the end of segregation was announced, so suddenly husbands and wives could move into the same little houses together. I think the script read, "Montage sequence: people moving backwards and forwards carrying furniture. Happiness", and so on.

'Now obviously, when you read about a montage sequence, you know that some composer is going to come in later and put in the beautiful underscore. I suggested to director Sophia Turkiewicz, a shot of a man carrying a portable gramophone with a record spinning on it. Bill Motzing composed his underscore, but it actually started off really scratchy and squeaky, as if it was all coming off a record player, and then it went into full-blown stereo. Integrating the sound and the image made the scene a lot more powerful.'

Even wardrobe items may be of interest to the sound recordist in pre-production. The rustling of a taffeta dress, for instance, can sound like an approaching bushfire!

On set, the recordist usually works with just one other person: the boom-swinger. Between them they set up a battery of microphones, stands, tape-recorders, boom-poles, clamps, gadgets, and often a mixer, together with the inevitable labyrinth of cables. Most of the equipment is personally owned and maintained by the recordist — a malfunctioning tape-recorder could destroy a day's work.

The boom-swinger holds a microphone on a pole as close as possible to the actor who is speaking, while keeping it out of frame.

This demands a familiarity with lighting (to avoid shadows from the boom), camera movement and lenses (to avoid intruding into frame), and the script (to keep the mircrophone trained on the appropriate speaker). The instant one actor has finished a line, the boom-swinger must be right on to the next speaker to catch that first syllable. If he or she is too slow, repair work in post-production may be necessary.

The difference a good boom-swinger makes may be defined in centimetres, as Syd Butterworth has found working with the likes of Sue Kerr:

'It's that ability to look at a lens and know precisely, for a given distance, where that lens is going to cut off. She might dip into frame during a rehearsal just to let the camera operator see where she is. The skill of the boom-operator can't be over exaggerated — it can make a considerable difference as to whether you get the shot or not — a fact which some producers don't seem to appreciate. I've heard one producer say to someone who was interested in coming on to a film crew, "Well, you could make the tea for a while, do a few messages, or hold the boom". In fact, it can make or mar a film as far as sound is concerned, and when you consider that sound carries the intelligence of the film...'

The boom-operator and the recordist operate as a close-knit team, and are interdependent in their effort to achieve good sound. While the boom-swinger is in the thick of the action, the recordist lurks off to the side with the tape-recorder. He monitors the intelligibility of the dialogue, the recording levels, and the amount of background noise, which may or may not interfere with the dialogue. As with the role of the continuity person in relation to the image, the sound recordist is also ensuring different print-takes will cut together without interference from sudden extraneous noises such as a dog barking, or a jet flying overhead.

In the process of striving to obtain clean, useable dialogue tracks, the sound recordist may actually affect the performance of the actors. Direct dealings with the performers depends on the relationship the recordist and the boom-swinger have with the director and the actors themselves.

'Some directors such as Di Drew are very easy to approach', said Butterworth. 'I think she respects what I do, and if I have something to say, she knows it's of consequence. Otherwise I tend to keep right out of the way and let things go.

'Listening as closely as I do, mispronunciation by an actor may be picked up by me, and not by others. I'll go and mention it, and it might be modified.

'Another thing is when, say, you do a master shot before the lunch break and the performance has taken a particular pattern, with a certain amount of energy in it. When you come back in the afternoon to complete the coverage on the scene, the energy might not be there — it may be a totally different performance. You remember that continuity aspect and mention it, because it would make it rather strange in cutting. But bringing the fact to the actor's attention has to be done in such a way that it doesn't give offence.'

'It's all a matter of timing', Mark Lewis commented. 'You know that between takes an actor is going to be jumped on by Make-up, Wardrobe, the camera department, and every other man and his dog. Generally, I like to get the last word in so they remember it, like, "Bring your voice up".'

The crusade for intelligibility must be tempered with discretion, to avoid compromising performance in the quest for technical perfection.

'One example of that', recalled Lewis, 'was Gosia Dobrowolska in *Silver City*. It was her first big film and she wasn't very easy to understand. I told the director that this was a major problem; that it was no good having her looking right and acting right if you couldn't understand her. It wasn't something you could clear up easily in post-sync either, so I really tried to make sure she was intelligible in every take.'

To the exasperation of other members of the crew, Lewis often asked for take after take to try and catch that elusive intelligibility.

'The only problem was that I found it did affect performance in some cases, and that's where you have to draw the line. There was one classic example where she said something like "forget-inden". I told her I didn't understand what she was saying, so she would try and enunciate it: "for-get-it-then", which robbed the performance of so much, it just sounded so wooden. We sort of compromised, so she was half understandable.'

Gosia's Polish accent aside, mumbling actors create the same dilemma. All the recordist can do is keep asking for more takes. The director will not usually raise any objections, although Lewis ran into problems with Dusan Makaveyev on *Coca-Cola-Kid*. The Hungarian director's own English was so strongly accented, he didn't know when someone was mumbling...

If poor speakers are a burden, it follows that good ones are a delight. Syd Butterworth revelled in recording *Travelling North*:

'A person like Leo McKern is marvellous to work with because he has a very clear speaking voice. He's a stage artist and he can be heard in very, very disadvantageous surroundings and very poor conditions.'

Another way in which the sound recordist may affect performance is by reminding actors of the context in which they are working. Lewis's example was once again drawn from *Silver City*:

'We had a scene in the back of an army truck driving along a dirt road. It was shot at the back of the studio, with the grips underneath rocking it up and down. The actors were just talking normally, so I told them I'd been in an army truck and you have to yell at the person you're sitting next to for them to hear you. I ended up with eight actors all yelling at one another, and all saying, "It's not going to work. I hate this".

'The next day, I took the truck for a drive and recorded the back of it. As soon as you put that wonderful, loud army truck sound with the actors shouting above one another, it worked like a treat.'

The same principle applies to something like a noisy pub scene. The background action in such scenes (extras talking and drinking, the band playing, glasses clinking, etc.) is all mimed during the takes in order to obtain clear dialogue. The actors may converse at normal levels rather than allow for the pandemonium that will be added later. When the dialogue has been completed the recordist will ask the first assistant for a few minutes of action by the extras alone. This material could be drawn from a sound effects library by the sound editor, but the criteria that make location dialogue preferable will apply.

If a line of dialogue is interrupted by a dog barking for example, rather than doing another take or having to post-sync it, the recordist may tape several wild lines. The actors repeat the relevant line several times on the spot, and at least one of these wild lines can be made to fit the lip movement of the print take.

In addition to recording dialogue, the recordist will also supply the sound editor with a mass of atmosphere tracks to be woven into the texture of the final soundtrack. While making *The Challenge* mini-series about the America's Cup, Mark Lewis used his lunch-hour to tape such things as the hammering in a shipyard, the wash of the ocean, and whatever else may have contributed to the aural milieu outside the offices of the Bond Syndicate. These atmosphere tracks were then played under the dialogue occurring in the offices, to intensify the illusion of reality.

'*Burke and Wills* was very good for the surround tracks', Syd Butterworth remarked. 'There were huge changes in location, from right up north in the Gulf country around Darwin, back down to Mildura and several weeks out at Cooper's Creek. And each area had its own specific sound.'

On this kind of film the sound recordist must be aware of where studio footage cuts into location material, so he can ensure there are atmosphere tracks to lay under the studio scenes.

'There was a scene on the banks of a river at Mildura', said Syd, 'with a night atmosphere, and King [Matthew Fargher] and Wills [Nigel Havers] talking inside a tent. You wouldn't believe that interior was done on the stage at the Regent Theatre in Sydney with traffic outside. The tracks that were played subtly as a background were recorded at Mildura.'

On the surface, a good sound recordist would seem to be someone who requires the least amount of post-syncing, but there have been times where Mark Lewis has suggested post-syncing a scene for purely artistic reasons. This happened in *Monkey Grip*, in which director Ken Cameron was keen to preserve the subjective, highly personal nature of Helen Garner's story.

'I suggested to Ken, before we'd even looked at locations, that it might be a good idea to post-sync the love-making scenes. Without any background sound whatsoever you can get that really warm, bassy, lovely breathing sound, that makes it very intimate, very subjective — 'in the head'. Nora [Noni Hazlehurst] was so obsessed with Javo [Colin Friels] that if a plane crashed outside the window when she was making love to him, she wouldn't hear it.

'In fact, when we shot the two love-making scenes, the sound was fine. But you still had that low traffic rumble, or whatever's just naturally there, outside. The whole idea was to get rid of any extraneous sound, so we did post-sync one of the scenes.'

With the completion of the shoot, the sound recordist's job is usually over. On rare occasions he may be invited to participate in post-production, something Lewis would like to do more frequently because no one knows better what is on those thousands upon thousands of feet of tape. Butterworth saw it as a possible source of conflict, and would rather keep clear:

'I usually contact the dubbing editor and tell them to give me a ring if they need anything. Beyond that, I am employed to do location recording, and there are other people employed to do sound editing and mixing, and they should be left to do their job. You should be able to rely on them to do a job that complements each person's work.'

Producer Sue Milliken, director Bruce Beresford, first assistant director Mark Egerton, continuity person Jo Weeks, director of photography Don McAlpine (obscured) and focus puller Warwick Field on location for *The Fringe Dwellers*. *Photo by Robert McFarlane, courtesy of Fringe Dwellers Productions Pty Ltd.*

8

Cutting Remarks

THE CONTINUITY PERSON

When Pam Willis joined the long-running serial *Bellbird* as a so-called 'script assistant', it looked as though she had fallen into a relaxing, paid holiday. No one seemed to talk much about continuity.

'The other girl told me that it was really easy. You just wrote down the shots and watched the cigarettes and candles. As we were filming in the bush there weren't any cigarettes or candles, so I thought it was a piece of cake!

'After watching for candles in the bush for some time, the editor called us both in one day and said, "Look girls, I can't cut this together very well. There are some things that you should know about head-turns, eyelines and things like that, which you should actually watch for. It would make my job much easier if you would watch the speed that someone's head turns in a wide-shot, and match it in a close-up, and watch whether their collars are up or down in the wide-shot, and match that to the close-up".

'We didn't know any of that. No one had taught us. We were off having a lovely time just writing all the shots down.'

The role of Continuity (know as script supervisor in the USA) is much broader in scope than even some directors appreciate. As the editor's eyes on set, they must ensure that nothing will unintentionally jar the audience's concentration: that there are no lapses in continuity from one shot to the next in relation to hair, make-up, wardrobe, props, and action so that the shots will cut together and that all necessary action has been shot.

The continuity person is first brought on about a month or so before the shoot to time the script. He or she will read all the dialogue and visualise all the action, and armed with a stopwatch, arrive at a fairly accurate running time for the script as it stands. At the same time, a day breakdown is prepared. The script is divided into script days, so that wardrobe will know when to change an actor's clothes, and the art department will know when props and decor — a bowl of flowers, for instance — will change or deteriorate.

These tasks completed, there will be a period off the payroll until a week or two before the end of pre-production when it is time to attend any rehearsals. At this time the script is broken down in detail.

'If someone is in a fight', explained Pam Willis, 'and they get a black eye in scene forty-seven, then, in discussion with the director you might decide that the black eye lasts until scene fifty-seven. So I make a note of it in every intervening scene, because when you are shooting out of sequence and you hit scene fifty-three one day, you need that reminder.'

Similarly, details concerning the props will be mapped out scene by scene: anything from the fate of hand luggage to the life-span of a dent in a car. This process may also reveal any inconsistencies or inaccuracies with time lapses within the script itself, which the director must remedy if there is no sound explanation for them.

Participation in rehearsals may amount to nothing more than noting script changes, or, as once happened to Jo Weeks, it may extend as far as actually running a rehearsal for a director who was absent through illness. As monotonous as it may sometimes be, attendance at rehearsals provides vital information for later use, such as an insight into how a director perceives a given character and what is expected from the actor's performance. Subsequently, if this performace is missing on the set, the continuity person may remind the director of what was being sought.

'When they've worked it all out', said Willis, 'and they're in a relaxed sort of rehearsal mode, you get a timing for each scene. That gives you a check, and if the performance becomes twice as long on set, you can tell the director who can then say, "Let's get back to the energy we had in rehearsal".'

Continuity may also be lumbered with reading the lines of absent actors, a task some do not relish at all. The first time Jo Weeks was ever asked to do this, on an episode of *Homicide*, she was politely told her performance was 'like extracting teeth from a dog'. She has shunned this chore ever since.

On set, the continuity person will generally be found perched on a collapsible stool as near as possible to the camera in order to identify what the lens is 'seeing'. Scripts, stopwatch, polaroid camera and note-pad are essential.

In addition to a complete master script, copies of the individual scenes to be shot that day are required so that the camera coverage may be marked up on them for the editor. This provides the editor with an instant guide to the different shots used to cover each piece of action or line of dialogue.

The stopwatch is in constant use, both to keep track of performance pacing, and to provide the production office with figures for endless computations about screen-time shot/against stock used/against time spent.

These days the polaroid camera is so central to the job, that it is difficult to imagine life without it. To cut down on the number of polaroids taken, Continuity often acts as photographer for Props, Hair, Make-up and Wardrobe. The positions of actors and props are photographed in each master set-up. Then if, say, during the course of shooting a close-up a coffee table is moved to accommodate the camera, the polaroid is there as a double check of the exact spot to reposition it. Similarly, the props department may request a polaroid of the table top, showing the placement of ashtrays, glasses, etc, which would be crucial were a pick-up shot called for later in the shoot.

There is a constant need for note-taking: timings, director's comments, preferred takes, lenses and filters used, and so on, which Continuity must somehow find time to type up during a day's shooting.

Whenever there are multiple takes of a given scene, it falls on Continuity to keep track of the director's reactions to each take, and to be able to remind him of the nuances of each one. At the end of the day everything is double-checked with the clapper/loader and the sound recordist to make sure that their print-takes correspond with the director's wishes.

'When you work with a new director', Pam Willis observed, 'it always takes a week or so to prove your worth. The first week is the hardest week because the director thinks, "Who is the little fly that keeps buzzing around my ears, suggesting things?" Once you have proved that you know what you're doing, then they tend to trust you a bit more. By the end of it, they are coming up to you and asking if they have forgotten anything. It's when they start trusting you that the job really takes off.'

As Jenny Quigley has found, however, some directors just never come to grips with how to make use of this 'little fly':

'One director in particular, just didn't use me. He didn't know why I was there. He thought that I was just an appendage that he had to cope with, to draw him up on any errors that he might make. It seems to me that the less experienced a director is, the less input I can have, which sounds crazy. But the more experienced the director, the more he knows the value of his continuity person.'

Continuity must be on the look-out for any line-crosses that may occur. If a shot of actor A establishes him looking left-to-right while talking to actor B, then it is essential that actor B's eyeline is right-to-left, so that when the two single shots are cut together, they appear to be talking to one another. If a car chase has been established as moving from right to left, a sudden cut to the leading vehicle moving left-to-right may well give the audience the impression that the two vehicles are on a collision course! Failure to adhere to this principle is known as 'crossing the line'.

The basic principle is to preserve the internal geography of a scene, so that wherever the camera shoots from, the subjects are seen to be facing or moving in a direction which is logical and consistent with the previous shots. However, even though 'thou shalt not cross the line' is a fundamental law of filmmaking, a director may often be too involved in supervising performance to realise the error, while others are unsure of the ground rules. Pam Willis:

'You keep watching the director. If he has a viewfinder, you can see where he's sorting out his shots. If you see him walking over there, when you know that the line of action is over here, then you say, "Excuse me, but if you go over there you are going to cross the line. Wouldn't it be nice if we did the shot from over here?" You try and nip it in the bud and stop the whole camera department moving, so the director doesn't make a mistake and make himself look like an idiot.'

Depending on the director, opportunities may also arise to make suggestions about coverage. It may be mentioning a line of dialogue that has not been covered in close-up, or, as Pam Willis recounted, pointing out something of interest in the set-up:

'In *Fragments of War — The Story of Damien Parer*, we did a scene in a Greek club, and there happened to be an extra who had worry beads. I said to John Duigan, "Don't you think a shot of him would be really good?" John had been doing something else and hadn't seen him and in the end he started a whole master-shot off with this guy and his worry beads.'

Even under normal shooting conditions, the time taken to reposition the camera and lights for a new angle on a scene can be anywhere from ten minutes to a matter of hours. During this period of waiting, the actors may forget exactly what they did in the previous set-up, or in the master-shot for the scene. Thus the continuity person must act as a sort of memory bank for the cast. In fact, Continuity is one of the few people on set allowed direct access to the actors. Pam Willis again:

'You've got to strike up a good rapport with the actors, make them trust you, and not bother them with silly bits and pieces, but rather pick out the important things to tell them. You can't go up to them like a sergeant-major and say, "Do that and that and that". But, by the same token, you've got to tell them what they did, so that they'll remember and do it again.'

The continuity person must hastily arrive at a judgement about how much information an actor can assimilate without their comments throwing the performance. Some very accomplished actors can pay meticulous attention to their own continuity without their acting suffering in the slightest. For others, even a gentle reminder from the continuity person may be sufficient to unsettle them. Naturally, this is more likely with young or very inexperienced actors.

Jenny Quigley looked after continuity on a television special of Bob Dylan in concert, directed by Gillian Armstrong. Some pick-up shots were required to be cut into the concert material.

'I had to go up to him and say, "Actually, Bob, you put your sunglasses down when you finished that bar, and there you picked up your guitar". He said, "Oh, really? Did I take my sunglasses off there?" And I said, "Yeah, well, that is what you did in the concert, and that is what we're matching it to".'

Jo Weeks worked on *The Fringe Dwellers* with an entire cast of first-time actors:

"You'd tell someone that they transferred their glass to their left hand and shook hands with their right, and they just couldn't do it. It was really difficult. The more so because to match the light and the weather, we had parts of individual scenes shot over eight weeks, with gaps of four weeks between shots sometimes.'

Careful He Might Hear You centred around the character of PS, played by seven-year-old Nicholas Gledhill. Pam Willis:

'He was a precocious sort of child, but he listened to me and was actually quite good at continuity. He trusted the director Carl Schultz, and was with him a lot. In between takes, he was sitting on Carl's knee and chatting to him. So it was sometimes harder to get to Carl than normal. At the same time, you didn't want to break up that relationship because it was very important for Carl to have that bond with Nicholas, in order to get a performance out of him.'

Aside from the experience or competence of the actors, a variety of situations can cause headaches for the continuity person. On *Rebel*, Jo Weeks had the assistance of a choreographer during the musical numbers, so that if a shot was picked up in the middle of a song, there was someone who could help identify the actors' positions. For the opulent mini-series, *Melba*, Jo's 'script' was sometimes a music score and an Italian libretto, upon which she had to try and base her notes on the actors' movements.

'Dinner parties are the worst scenes', she said. 'They are a nightmare unless the director has really got it down pat. You could spend a week covering all the action going on around a table, and making sure who is looking at who, and that all the screen directions are right. And there's also the eating. Did they have a pea on their fork, or a lump of meat?

'You can streamline it by knowing the cutting points. Then you don't have to watch everything; you can't watch everything, anyway.'

Both Jo Weeks and Pam Willis worked on the mini-series *Bodyline*, about the infamous cricket tests between Australia and England in the 1930s. Jo was looking after continuity on the second unit, which was filming the cricketing scenes, while Pam was doing the main unit. With no opportunity to exchange information, maintaining continuity between the main unit and the second unit was extremely difficult.

'Second unit did the cricketing coverage until the players started to walk off the field', explained Willis. 'On main unit we were picking them up walking off the field and into the pavillion. Things like whether they had their hats and gloves on or off were a nightmare.'

Because of the sheer volume of footage and length of shoots, mini-series seem to create extra problems for Continuity, but none more than *The Challenge*, the epic story of Australia's victory in the America's Cup.

'It was pretty silly', recalled Pam Willis, 'because it was being filmed on a twelve-metre yacht off Perth for a month, they didn't want to take me — "Sorry, no room for girls". (Apart from anything else, there were no loos on board.) The Bond camp said they could only take six people on board, so I was ensconced on *Black Swan*, the tender.

'The first morning, off I went and set myself up on the bridge, with binoculars and a walkie-talkie to the focus puller. They couldn't take a clapper/loader, so there was no paperwork. I was supposed to do all the paperwork over the walkie-talkie.

'So I had the script on my knees, the binoculars, and the walkie-talkie, and I'm saying to the driver of the *Black Swan*, "Get closer, I can't see". And the sound department is saying, "Get that tender away. It's too noisy".

'It was all to be integrated with stock footage of the actual races. We only had two yachts: the real *Australia II*, and a South Australian yacht painted as *Liberty*, with the right sails. When they were racing other yachts we had to integrate the stock footage, and that meant matching sails and spinnakers.

'Then we found out that the wardrobe department didn't have the right information about the wardrobe. They'd put them in wet-weather gear, whereas in fact, the guys were just wearing anything. So my walkie-talkie was going mad: "What are they wearing? What's the weather like?" We had to match the weather and the seas as well.

'Then, before the first slate was actually shot, this rubber-ducky came screeching over from *Australia II*, about half a mile away and I was told to get on. Once on board *Australia II*, I never got off. They decided it was a bit too hard to work with a walkie-talkie.'

At rushes, if the editor is present, Continuity may have little more to do than confirm that all the right takes have been printed. If the crew are out of town on location, and the editor is back in the city, Continuity must glean as much information as possible from the director to pass on to the editor. The cutting order for a given scene will have been taken down by Continuity and passed on to the editor.

The continuity person is continually having to criticise the work of other departments. Jo Weeks again:

'You could get really paranoid about it, because it is such a negative area. Everyone is friends on set, but your job is to say to the hairdresser for example, "No, I don't think that matches", and it's *their* profession. You are always telling props something is not right. You're always writing down who did what wrong, and double checking on everyone's job. As Continuity, you are the last cover before it goes on to celluloid.'

As Jenny Quigley noted, this results in a degree of awareness of what everyone is doing on set that would only be matched by the first assistant director:

'If the producer walks on set, you are sometimes the first person they ask for an idea of how things are going, which is because of this constant process of double checking. Continuity pulls all the departments together on set — make-up, wardrobe, props, even the camera department — to make sure the film cuts together.'

Editor John Scott. *Photo by Jim Sheldon.*

9

Celluloid Sculptor

THE EDITOR

The popular conception of outstanding editing is epitomised by fast-moving scenes in action films such as the *Mad Max* sagas. In fact, most awards for editing go to films which have dazzled the judges with a myriad of rapid cuts. Rarely are they as glowing in their response to something that is slower paced and meticulously edited, even though it may have been infinitely more difficult to piece together than a tumultuous action movie. The immense contribution of the editor is hidden from the audience.

Next to the producer, the director, and possibly the writer, the editor generally has the longest association with a given project. He or she joins the crew at the tail end of pre-production and is then working every day until the final mix is completed. It all adds up to a minimum of six months and can stretch out to the ten months that Nick Beauman worked on *Mrs Soffel* with Gillian Armstrong.

During shooting, the rushes which are sent to the laboratory each day are in the form of exposed negative, carefully canned and loaded by the clapper/loader. The lab develops the exposed negative each night, and from this strikes a positive copy known as a workprint. The negative is then held in safety for the Neg Matchers to use once a final cut of the entire film is completed.

The assistant editor synchronises the appropriate sound with the work print for the rushes screenings.

This workprint becomes the primary tool of the editor. It can be cut up and handled with impunity as it is independent of the original negative.

These days the majority of editors prefer to do most of their work using an editing flatbed: a machine the size of a small dining table, with a picture screen and loud speaker mounted at the back. The workprint and separate magnetic sound tracks are placed onto plates on the left hand side of the machine and threaded through a system of cogs which feed the material horizontally across the table to take-up plates on the other side. The image and the sound can be played simultaneously at normal speed, high speed, backwards, or even one frame at a time.

Using a grease pencil, the editor will make a mark directly onto the workprint at the exact frame where he wishes to make a splice. The workprint is then physically cut using a splicer with a small guillotine-like action, and reassembled using clear splicing tape. Should the cut be changed, the splicing tape is simply peeled off and another piece of tape applied.

There is an irony in the fact that the editor's role is largely to conceal his own handiwork. Each edit, or cut in the film, will be scrutinised to ensure that it does not disrupt the visual flow. Except where it is dramatically advantageous, a cut which draws attention to itself is generally considered shoddy. So the better the editor's execution, the less we are aware of his input. Yet the editor's creative contribution is immense.

'Editing it not taking out', said Beauman, 'it is putting together. It's a bit like sculpting. But whereas sculptors start off with a block which they whittle away at, we sort of build up a block, or build up the picture, and then we chip away at it, polish it, chip away, refine it, and smooth out the rough edges.'

Obviously this expertise is not acquired ovenight: most film editors have served a lengthy apprenticeship before being entrusted with a feature. The nature of this learning process may vary, the normal course being to spend several years as an assistant editor. Nick Beauman stepped sideways through the fairly exclusive door to the features cutting room via an extensive history of cutting television commercials.

'I learned a lot from commercials because you're telling stories in a very short space of time, and anything goes. There was a lot of convention tied into film editing in the old days like having to start a scene with a wide shot for example — and I think that's all gone out of the window. In my years in commercials, I had to try all sorts of weird and wonderful things, which I've sometimes been able to apply to my feature work. Certainly, using tricks that I've learned in commercials has enabled me to get out of problem situations at times.'

Beauman will still occasionally cut a television commercial, even though he is established as a leading features editor. This flexibility is a luxury in jobs that tend to be mutually exclusive. Both he and John Scott are freelance operators who must rely on producers or directors to contact them with offers of work. Having accepted a job, the editor may be asked for his views on the script. On one rather rare occasion, Beauman discovered that his opinion was not entirely welcome.

'I did a film called *The Earthling* and got off to a bad start with the director, Peter Collinson, whose only real claim to fame was *The Italian Job*. I was initially attracted because it was a big overseas production for that time [1980]. It was going to star William Holden and I thought cutting something with him in it would be pretty good fun.

'I wasn't thrilled by the script, which had Australian wildlife just crawling out of it. They had packs of wild dogs attacking people, and hot geysers, and lots of things that you just don't find here. I told the producer I was interested in doing it but I thought there were a few things in the script that were a bit dodgy. He said, "Fine, fine. We appreciate that we don't understand some aspects of Australia and maybe there'll be a problem in terms of believability. How about you put your thoughts down on paper and I'll pass them on to Peter. He'll be delighted to get your comments".

'Well, he wasn't delighted at all. He was livid. He accused me of trying to tell him how to direct his picture, and went right off the deep end. I told him that was the last thing I'd want to do, but I was just a bit concerned about some aspects of the script. His response was, "You do your job and I'll do mine".

'From that time on, I would never take on a film that I didn't feel some empathy for, because it's such a long time in an editor's life. If you're working on something you don't believe in, it's hard getting up every day and conning yourself that it's not as bad as it really is, which is what we were doing on *The Earthling*. You were telling yourself, "It's okay. Once we've trimmed it all up, and got a good music score, and done a good mix..." If it's not there at the script stage, it's not going to be there at the end.'

The degree of interaction between the editor and the director before shooting commences is largely dependant on the director. On some projects, the editor might be lucky to meet the director once or twice during pre-production. In other cases, the director may actually go through the script in detail with the editor, explaining how he plans to cover each scene. Even when a director is resolved on how he will shoot something, there may be room for suggestion from the editor, as John Scott explained:

'Let's say the scene is a car going off a bridge. The director may have decided on wide shots and close-ups of the car during the stunt, but he's forgotten a close-up of the driver's face. To me, as an editor, the most important thing is for the audience to be able to identify with the character. It's not about watching a car flying through the air, it's about being in the car yourself, which you achieve in editing via the face of the character. Especially in action, you need all the elements: hands on steering-wheel, feet on pedals; close-ups of every detail of the car and the driver at every moment. Then, with the correct juxtaposition of all those shots, an editor can create something that works.'

Unfortunately, due to the constraints of time, and the attitude of many directors, these consultations with the editor in pre-production are a rarity. Yet an experienced editor has a vastly greater knowledge of coverage than most directors.

'Directors don't spend a lot of time with other directors, either', observed Scott. 'I think it's probably true to say the editors spend more time with more directors, and know more about different filmmakers' ways of making films than anybody else on a picture. You know more about what you can do with coverage because you've seen it all before.'

Before shooting commences, the editor sets up his cutting room and hires his assistants. The number of assistants will vary between one and three, according to the budget. If there is the luxury of three people, during the shoot the first assistant editor will work directly with the editor, putting together scenes that the editor has marked up for cutting. The second assistant syncs up and prepares daily rushes for screening each evening. The third assistant catalogues and codes all the material. For the post-production phase, there would normally be only two assistants. The more assistants, the more time the editor has to experiment with cutting scenes in different ways.

The cutting room really opens for business on the second day of the shoot, when the editor receives developed footage from the first day. As Beauman has found, these daily rushes may or may not be accompanied by instructions from the director on how to assemble them:

'There are directors who know that if they go out there and do wide shots, two-shots and singles, the editor will make something out of it, but they don't really see it in their mind's eye. They don't know how it's going to turn out until the editor actually presents it to them. Then they say, "Oh, yeah, that works", or "Why don't you try that?", but I don't think they have a real vision. They're what I describe as formula directors.

'And then there are people like Gill Armstrong, who have a definite vision of the film; who think about transitions from one scene to another; who think about camera moves. If they move the camera around — which she does quite a lot — they think about how to get in and out of that, and the overall visual style, and so forth.'

It is at the screening of rushes each night during filming that the editor has an opportunity to pick the director's brains: which takes are preferred in terms of performance, and how a scene cuts together. For example the director may see the scene beginning with a wide shot and going to a mid-shot, or vice versa. Performance will also be a major factor in this decision-making.

'If you've got a good rapport with the director as I have with Gill', commented Beauman, 'then at the end of looking at a particular set-up, I'll say "Take two", and nine times out of ten she'll say, "Yes". Or she'll say, "I quite like that one as well", and then I'll say, "Well, I'll look at both of them again".'

Armed with the director's input, the editor can begin assembling a rough cut of each scene. This has the potential to reveal the biggest bugbear the editor faces: lack of coverage.

'Let's say it's a comedy', said Scott, 'and you've got a one minute scene which they've rehearsed, and know is funny. They don't want to waste any film — they want to do it all in one shot. Fine. They do it and it works, and it is funny. Everybody loves it at rushes.

'Further down the track when you put the film together, the scene, which has been very funny up until this point, can sit in the film and suddenly destroy the pace of the whole thing. An editor must have tools like close-ups, to be able to condense a scene, and not just be limited to starting it later or ending it earlier.

'Editing has a lot to do with pace and timing, and especially in comedy, that's very tricky. I'll always argue that the director should get more than one shot. Then I can make sure the sequence works in the total film and not just as an isolated scene. I think it's fair to argue that when you're shooting a film, the cheapest commodity is the stock itself. Having so many crew standing by, the cast standing by, and with all the equipment, it's much better to roll the cameras, and shoot a bit more film. Inevitably you will end up using most of everything you shoot. Even if it's only for moments, it's always useful. On the other hand, you've got to be reasonable about it, because quite often it's just not practical to be able to get the coverage within the budget, or within the time. On a low budget film where everything is tight you have to try and work out where you are going to need the coverage most, such as in difficult scenes, or scenes that are more important to the story or character development.'

Nick Beauman has enjoyed a long and fruitful association with Gillian Armstrong, going back to *The Singer and the Dancer* in 1976.

'On *High Tide*, I was away on location the whole time. If I felt there was a problem with a scene I would talk to her about it. I might suggest she come and have a look at it or I might suggest such-and-such a shot would help. In fact, she didn't see a great deal of my work on location because I think we've got to that stage where if I don't say anything she knows there's not going to be a problem. Even if I haven't cut the scene exactly the way she might like it, at least she knows, and I know, that we can do that at a later stage, together.

'I almost instinctively know whether she's going to like what I've done with a scene or not. It's a bit like me with an assistant, I suppose: if I know that the assistant understands the way I operate, then it's going to speed up the process all the way down the line.'

Problems of coverage aside, a day or two after the editor and director have discussed a scene at rushes, a rough cut will be ready for the director to look at. John Scott:

'You'll be wanting to get his impressions of what you've just done. Usually, what happens is that the director will suggest another way, and then you'll think of something slightly different again. When there's a perfect working relationship between the director and the editor, they feed off each other, and the material just keeps on improving. You're looking at rushes daily, so as you see the film developing, you're in a position to argue for and talk about what's working, what's not working, and what to do about it.

'That's why you cut so much while the film is being shot. You've still got a chance to re-shoot something, or pick something up for it, because the crew's all still there. I will ask for something additional to be shot if there's some sort of problem.

The editor learns how each scene has been covered via the script mark-up prepared for him by the continuity person who, ideally, ensures that the editor can make a cut wherever he chooses without being hindered by problems of mismatched continuity. However, when problems do arise, the editor can sometimes work around them, as Scott explained:

'I pass you a glass and you take it with your left hand in one shot, and your right hand in another. If I cut it at a certain point in the action, nobody will ever notice that it's a different hand that it's been taken by, because the smoothness of the action is so deceiving. As an editor you'll see it, but an audience never gets that opportunity to go backwards and forwards. As long as it's smooth, it won't be that obvious that something's wrong. The mind can't jump back to the previous frame.'

'That's the great tool that an editor has', echoed Beauman. 'A cut happens so quickly and an audience doesn't know when it's going to happen. If it's bad, you might say that there was something funny about that, but unless you go back and look at it, you won't be able to say what it was.

'I think you expect continuity problems. Continuity's task is pretty hard, and occasionally things will be missed, although I don't think I've ever done a film where I could say that Continuity was absolutely hopeless and made my job a nightmare. Generally speaking, I have a number of different shots for each scene so that if I do get a problem, I can move onto another shot to overcome it.'

With the completion of shooting, the film, for better or for worse, exists as a celluloid entity, and the original script is little more than an historical document.

'It doesn't matter what the intention *was* any more', said Scott. 'Reality is what's on celluloid. It doesn't matter if it says in the script that it's supposed to have this meaning. If the celluloid isn't giving that meaning, then an editor has to make it give its own meaning. It's quite a different thing and you have to be objective. Quite often, what was intended may not be there, or different shades of what was meant might be apparent.

'I remember when Makaveyev was talking to me about cutting *Coca-Cola Kid*, he asked me if I had a high regard for the script on a film. I told him I had none at all, which pleased him. Apparently he'd worked with one of Ingmar Bergman's editors who wouldn't let Makaveyev change his own film because it wasn't what was said in the script. He found that very frustrating.'

Similarly, Beauman may read the script two or three times before the film starts, but doesn't use it at all once he is cutting other than to refer to the coverage information the continuity person has marked up on it. He lets the existing footage tell him the story.

Beauman and Scott vary in their methods of assembling a first rough cut. Beauman favours cutting each individual scene fairly tightly, to get a clear impression of how the scenes are working. Scott prefers to assemble a complete rough cut as quickly as possible, to get a view of the overall structure. He will then go back and start working from the inside. Either way, both men prefer to assemble their own cut of the film before they begin chipping away at it in conjunction with the director. Beauman once again referred to his long-standing partnership with Gillian Armstrong:

'When the shoot is over, the process that we generally adopt is to go through a reel or two, and talk about that reel scene by scene: whether things are working, and if they're not, how they can be fixed. Then she'll go away, and we'll make a time for her to come back and look at the re-structure.'

Beauman will then piece together large slabs of the picture and Armstrong will then make suggestions or point out problems. This process embodying John Scott's earlier description of the perfect editor/director relationship. The pertinent point is that most of the hand-on work is done in isolation. An exception was *Starstruck*, for which some of the song sequences were assembled with Armstrong in constant attendance.

'In fact', reflected Beauman, 'it's a slow process if I've got to accommodate somebody else sitting there. I mean, if I'm there by myself, I make the decision about what I'm going to do. If I've got the director there, I've got to say, "Well, how about we do it this way? Do you agree with that?". I would rather discuss those kinds of decisions beforehand, and then say, "You go away and I'll do it. Then come back to have a look and see whether you're happy or not". I always do find it a bit inhibiting having somebody sitting around. It makes me feel slightly uptight, no matter how well I know the person. Just the fact that they're sitting there makes me start to wonder if I'm taking too long over these changes.'

While the constant presence of the director may be undesirable, regular input from that source is crucial to the editor, particularly regarding performance, as Nick Beauman explained:

'Sometimes Gill will want to go back and look at alternate takes of key performances in some particular scenes, just to make sure that I haven't overlooked something that was better. She'll say to me, "I think that line was better in Take Two". So we'll put it back up again, have a look, and yes, she might be right, or she'll say, "No, my memory's deceiving me".

'If she says "Take Two is the take for me", I won't deliberately go against that, unless I feel that there's very good reason for it. Or I'll say, "I used Take Two down to that point, but I thought she was a bit weak on the last line, so I went back to Take One". If an editor is going to go against the director, I think he has to have a very good reason for doing so. Ultimately, it's the director's decision.'

Nonetheless, in the director's absence, the editor is constantly making a multiplicity of decisions in relation to both performance and pacing which affect the end product. John Scott:

'If you've got two people in conversation, you have to be able to pick the precise moment to cut from one person to the other, and to get eye contact going between the two people. You have to know when to cut to the reaction of the other person. You watch the material very carefully, and begin to understand the flow of the performances — both the active person, who is talking, and the passive person, who is listening — so you're able to create a cutting pattern that starts to tell what's going on between those two people. That's a very interesting and very difficult thing to do. And that can have a lot of influence on how a scene will work.'

Nick Beauman also used the example of a two-way conversation, of which there are four printed takes:

'Just because I've selected Take Two of one person, and Take Four for the other, I won't just stick with those. At the time I want to go away to the other person for a particular line, he might be weak on that line. So I'll look at the other takes, and see if perhaps he was stronger on that line in one of them. Actors probably don't realise how their performances are manipulated by the editor. We take a bit from here and a bit from there, and meld it all together.'

Because these decisions are constantly being made, the editor must be attuned to the nuances of the art of acting. Mistakes by an actor can create special problems for that actor and subsequently the editor. When an actor fluffs a line, a common procedure is for the director to call for a 'pick-up', that is, the scene is picked up a couple of lines before the mistake occured. Beauman again:

'I don't believe that actors can just pick up a line. I don't think they ever really get the flow of their performance unless they start from the beginning. I know that the amount of footage that Gill used to use was often a source of concern to the producers, because she invariably insisted on going from top to bottom in a scene. But I think in terms of performance, it always pays off. It avoids the timing of the actor's delivery being out.'

John Scott expanded on the relationship between performance and pacing in the editor's work by comparing the role of the film actor with that of the stage actor:

'With theatre, an actor can modify his performance according to how the audience is reacting each night. With film, you're locked into the one performance every night. This is where editing comes in: an editor has to move an audience and change an audience with his timing. He drags things out when he wants to, or takes things away before they're fully realised, keeping the audience alive.

'I find comedy probably the most difficult to put together, because you've always got to be one jump ahead of the audience, never letting them finish a laugh before you move onto the next one. The thriller is the other exciting one to put together: to always keep one step ahead of the audience; always keep them guessing.'

Once again, the editor is at the mercy of the material the director supplies. Nick Beauman recalled a scene in *Mrs Soffel* in which the husband and wife are dining together:

'It starts with a high angle shot, and then the camera tracks down and goes into a two-shot, holds on the two-shot, and then pulls back out again. So that's a one shot scene. But because Gill was not a hundred percent sure whether it would seem too slow a moment at that particular point in the film when the whole thing was cut together, she also did some additional coverage. I cut it both ways. But I think generally speaking, the subject matter tends to dictate how the film might be cut. If you were doing a film like *Bullitt*, you wouldn't put in slow tracking shots. You'd try to make it as racy as hell.

'Often, you make a change to something, and then look at it and realise that because you've stepped up the tempo of that scene, you've in turn affected the tempo of some of the other scenes around it. So what appears to be a relatively simple thing, ends up being much more complex because it affects the overall flow and rhythm of the film.'

Both men find the cutting process entirely intuitive — a matter of feeling the flow of each scene, and its relationship to the whole. Beauman was adamant that tight deadlines help in this process. He has found that an abundance of time results in him thinking about the cuts too much, agonising over which way to go.

During the three months or so of post-production that the picture editing process can take, the film may be screened for selected audiences, just to make sure the intuition has not gone rusty in the cutting room.

'Suddenly, just by being in the theatre with other people around, you can feel what they're feeling, and you start to see the film for the first time again,' affirmed Scott. 'The presence of other people makes you look at it in a different way, and you start to see what's going wrong. You invite people to these screenings whom you trust, who you know will be honest and who, hopefully, will be able to tell you what's wrong. Somebody might tell you that something is not working, and what you should do. They might be wrong about what you should do, but right that it isn't working. You can work out what to do.'

One of the most complex films John Scott has edited was *Newsfront*, which combined colour sequences with black and white, and 1950s newsreel footage with fictional newsreel footage.

'The black and white material was specifically shot to look like a newsreel in its framings. We watched hundreds of newsreels and quite often they were crudely cut, because they were so hurried. So part of the process was to be able to imitate that crude cutting, and not polish things. It's actually very hard to go back and make the same little rough bits and pieces here and there, and have things slightly a-rhythmical. You get rhythms in newsreels that follow patterns: you pull out a piece of film from your nose to your hand, and that's three feet, so that's good for a close-up; you double that, and it's good for a wide shot. I don't think I ever actually measured it out by hand, but we re-cut all the newsreels, and tried to do it in the same style, and to integrate our own footage in the same style. That was fascinating.

'Quite often in newsreels, shots 'cross the line', because they're done very quickly. Somebody might be looking one way, then you see their point-of-view and it seems to be in the wrong direction. I found that doing things like that — using shots that didn't really go together — gave it a flavour of being authentic.

'During the last weeks of post-production, we went off to Canberra to get more newsreel footage. We were told by the producers that we couldn't go because there was no more money, but we went anyway. That's when we found, by accident — it wasn't catalogued — Chico Marx playing *Waltzing Matilda*, which opens the film. It was just by constant searching that we found that. Going to the libraries and searching through all this material was another excitement of the film.

'So much of the editing craft was offered by that film because of the nature of it; so it was complex. We were able to use just about every editing device, every editing trick, and every editing style in one film, which is rare.

'After the fine cut and before the mix, I like to lay up all the music and be heavily involved in that side of a film. With *Newsfront*, the newsreels were even scored in the original style. It was a very exciting film to work on', said Scott.

Music can be vitally important to the editor's work, reinforcing his concepts of rhythm and flow within the film. Both Beauman and Scott are in the habit of laying up existing recorded music to suit the film, while they are working on it.

'This is to enhance a scene', Beauman explained, 'or to add emotion, or just to give it additional flavour. Sometimes too, it gives you a sense of timing for a scene. Music can make an enormous difference to the pacing.

'I remember when reading *High Tide*, the big scene on the beach made me think of a Supertramp track called *Crime of the Century*. I took a lot of cassettes away with me on location and when I cut the sequences down, I put the cassette on, and it just worked like a dream. When we got the composer in to see the film we took all the music out because we felt we didn't want to influence his creative contribution. But for that particular scene he wasn't able to create the same feeling we were getting from the Supertramp track, so we finally did play it to him, and then he got it.'

At the same time that the composer is toiling away over a hot keyboard, the sound editor is laying up tracks in the cutting room. Generally speaking, the editor will have had considerable say in the choice of sound editor, and being head of the editing department, will oversee the work.

The editor will also be liaising constantly with the laboratory throughout the post-production phase. John Scott:

'If you're doing opticals or special effects, or any special grading like day-for-night, anything that's surreal, a high contrast process or a laboratory optical effect, you'll do a lot of tests, and see a lot of variations. You'll start choosing the ones that work, and they'll be cut into the film in their first rough-graded forms, waiting for the final grading involving the DOP.'

As the picture editing nears completion, differences of opinion may become more overt, occasionally drawing the editor into a crossfire between the director and the producer.

'Often the director's problem is that it's hard to be ruthless', commented Beauman. 'They get emotionally attached to the scene because they made the crew carry a crane up a five hundred foot mountain and work five hours overtime to get the shot. Then the editor comes along and says, "Drop it. We don't need it". On the whole, I think most directors know they can't let these sort of things influence them. I think less experienced filmmakers sometimes tend to hold on to things. They're not as disciplined.'

John Scott concurred: 'You'll find that you're suggesting we drop the director's favourite shot, or maybe it's your favourite shot, and everyone else wants to drop it. I don't see much difference in the roles of editor and director. To me, it's just two filmmakers on a film. Each one is there to help the other, and the film's what's important. The whole editing process becomes a thing of cleansing a film down to its real performance and its real meaning.

'I suppose one of the best things that can happen in the cinema is to move an audience emotionally in some way, whether it's to make them laugh, make them cry, make them frightened, or make them sad. That's the magic of filmmaking. And I suppose editing contributes to that, along with a script, soundtrack, performances, sets, direction, cinematography and music. Every little aspect of filmmaking is part of the film. It's a collective medium. Everybody's work makes the film work.'

Phil Heywood and sound mixer Peter Fenton at the mixing desk. *Photo courtesy of Colorfilm Pty Ltd.*

10

Aural Architects

THE SOUND EDITOR
and
THE MIXER

Going to the movies and closing your eyes may sound like a daft thing to do, but it will open your ears to the myriad subtleties and complexities of the soundtrack. A subliminal aural assault is taking place, which, together with the dialogue and the music, weaves spells as powerful as the moving pictures themselves.

'There has always been a shortage of good dubbing editors in Australia, and I think that's because they get treated rather shabbily, so either they burn out, or they think, "I'm not going to go on doing this. It's too hard, and I'm not getting the respect for the time and for the job that I deserve". They don't get a fair deal. They're always squeezed, because they're locked in to a mixing date. Quite often, the picture editing process goes over time, so the amount they've been given to do their jobs gets condensed even further. Then they're working seven days a week, twenty-four hours a day, for not wonderful money.'

This gloomy sketch of the position of the sound (or dubbing) editor was drawn by picture editor Nick Beauman. Probably nowhere else in Australian filmmaking is the ratio of creative input to recognition so disparate, although the tide may be turning. Gillian Armstrong:

'I feel it's great that dubbing editors are seeing themselves more and more as creators, and are really thinking about sound as a tapestry.'

The sound editor is chosen by the picture editor or the director, and their main work commences when a fine cut of the film exists. Greg Bell likes to have at least eight weeks to complete the soundtrack before the final mix. This was the case on *Echoes of Paradise*, for example, on which his crew consisted of a dialogue editor with an assistant, and an effects editor with an assistant. Bell himself still performed about half of each task, and supervised the rest.

The first job is to clean up the dialogue tracks, eliminating lisps, lip-smacks, noises from the camera dolly, and all other extraneous sound which may distract the audience, and weaken the illusion.

Then it is necessary to determine what dialogue, if any, needs post-syncing or re-voicing. This may be necessary because the dialogue is not clear enough — due to poor diction, for example — or because of unwanted and unavoidable noise at the time of shooting. The film with the dialogue tracks is screened in a mixing theatre, and the mixer treats it electronically in various ways to see what can be fixed up. The director may decide that some parts that seem to need post-syncing would be too difficult for the actors to pull off, perhaps because the scene is heavily emotional, or the dialogue overlaps or whatever. The possibility of masking unwanted sounds with extra effects or music may even be considered. Occasionally, the composer is present at this screening.

During post-syncing, the sound editor may have a direct impact on the actors' performances. The process usually takes place in a post-sync theatre, which is a small recording studio with projection facilities. These days a computer is programmed with the start and finish points of a specific piece of dialogue. It provides a visual cue on the screen and an audio cue in the actors' headphones. The actors also have the original dialogue in the headphones, so they can hear, as well as see, whether their lines are synchronised or not.

'Some actors are so nervous and terrified by the process', said Bell, 'that you've got to boost them up and knead them into shape. They have to know and trust the process, so they'll be comfortable in the theatre, confident and loose enough to be able to act again.

Some of them have had bad experiences with post-sync, where it's looked out of sync, and sounded awful. The performance has suffered, and the whole scene has lost its credibility. Phil Noyce and I have got a great system for working with difficult actors. We work like the cops, where he'll be the bad guy, and I'll be the good guy, or vice versa.

'There are other less experienced directors who prefer to leave the control of the performance up to me. They sit back, and I work with the actor totally. I'm always astonished when that happens, but it can be good. Some actors and I go into the theatre knowing exactly what we've got to do. We play off each other, and work the whole thing through, and the director might be a nuisance to us both.'

An ambivalent attitude on the part of some directors can extend beyond post-syncing to the whole process of creating the soundtrack. Bell:

'Some directors are really not sound-aware, and prefer not to get involved. They like the idea that they've hired a professional sound editor, so they can just wash their hands of it, and walk off. Also, I now find that I'm much more experienced in the filmmaking process than nearly all of the directors I work with. They've only made ten films; I've worked on hundreds. A lot of them get intimidated by that.

'I try and find *how* I can make them understand what I'm doing, so they can get involved. It's a lonely process if the director isn't involved. I hate those kind of jobs where they give you all the rolls of film and say, "You can work over there. We'll see you in six weeks at the mix." If you haven't got the support and involvement of the director and the production people, it's an awful job. It goes on for weeks, and no one's there. It's a self-discipline thing: it's so easy to get behind.

'I don't like them hanging around, but I do like to see the director every day, and tell him what I'm up to — whether the latest idea we talked about is going to work — and play them the results.'

Bell's criticism of directors extends even more vehemently to producers.

'Mostly they think you're trying to take them to the cleaners, because you're doing something they can't even see, and they don't believe it. They see all this money going into an empty hole, and they can't ever see any result. They just look at films, and think about the story. They don't have the fine tuning of the senses to realise what sound does: how it manipulates people, how effectively the Hollywood people use it, and how it is a large part of the storytelling process.'

Some films, such as *Echoes of Paradise*, are enormously complicated in their demands upon the sound editor. Two thirds of

Echoes was shot at Phuket in Thailand. The story concerned a woman, who, having fled from personal crises in Sydney, arrives in a tropical paradise, Unfortunately, the reality of Phuket was rather different:

'All you could hear were ducks, chickens, transistor radios, dogs, kids, motor-cycles, and the little tuk-tuk bus things they've got', Bell said ruefully. 'It was just a completely uncontrollable sound situation. So we had to throw out all of that original track and re-create it.

'I wanted this complete, exotic feeling, and was terrified because I didn't have a lot of Asian sounds in my library. Naturally enough, all the sounds are completely different from here, and they've got to sound different. You can't just put in any old birds, because people start to feel like they're back in Chatswood. They've got to feel this exotic thing, like they're in a really lovely, peaceful place.

'People who have seen the film kept saying what a beautiful place it was, and I'd think to myself that if they'd heard what it was really like, they'd be saying what a dog of a place it was.

'Another example was the New Zealand film, *Quiet Earth*, which was shot in an industrial part of town, with no sound-proofing whatsoever. It was set after the holocaust. Nothing was happening out there: no engines, no people; even the birds were dead. There was nothing that could create sound at all. So we had to rip the whole soundtrack out for every single shot, throw it away, and start again, to get that eerie feeling.'

Once the best possible dialogue tracks have been created, the sound editor lays up all the effects and atmosphere tracks. Not only the director, but also the picture editor may have some ideas to throw in here. Bell said he goes out of his way to milk as much information out of the latter as possible, because inevitably ideas have cropped up while they were cutting the film. Being so attuned to the pacing of the picture, the editor can also point out dull patches which need bolstering from the soundtrack. This is not to downplay the enormous input of a good director, as Bell outlined in relation to Phillip Noyce:

'Phillip and I talk the film through, and define each scene in terms of the story. We establish whether each scene is telling the story well or not; whether it needs a distracting sound, or a warm feeling, a cold feeling, or a violent edgy feeling.

'We don't talk that much about exactly what I'm going to use to do that, because a lot of those ideas to do with emotive sound are really determined by what you have. It's just like picture: you've got to actually have it on tape. On most films, there isn't a lot of time or money to create sound effects. I rely heavily on my own library — which is pretty extensive — pulling sounds out, and playing them with the picture. I don't necessarily do what I originally said I was going to do, because I might not have the right combination of sounds to actually make that sound-progression that we've discussed. But I keep in mind the emotional direction required.'

Effects make an immense contribution to the success of a movie. The story is continually reinforced by soundscape atmospheres, and the quality and scope of the soundscape helps generate the magic of a memorable night at the cinema. Contrary to what one might expect, these aural backdrops are more crucial in a gentle love story than they are in a full-blown action adventure. Long stretches of apparent quiet and intimacy give the sound editor ample scope to shift the mood of the audience. With a noisy film the riproaring dialogue and action are so dominant there is less scope or need for the sound editor to weave spells.

It is a paradox of the job that the sound editor does not hear his or her own work until the final mix. He laboriously creates the individual threads of sound, but the total texture of dozens of tracks can only be sampled in his mind — rather like a composer writing for a large orchestra, of which the mixer is the conductor.

'I liken it to architecture', said Bell. 'There's a lot of design involved, and then, when your job is over, the thing materialises.'

The sound editor may also lay up the music tracks, but as this work is more commonly executed by the picture editor, it is covered in Chapter 9. The final soundtrack, of course, is an interrelationship between dialogue, music, sound effects and atmosphere tracks. Bell thinks of the dialogue as the backbone of the soundtrack, while the music, effects, and atmospheres are like the flesh.

'The backbone has got to be audible to tell the story correctly. The story should not be interfered with by miscellaneous noises or strange background sounds which don't relate to the story and put you off the fact that the characters are supposed to be in this particular place.

'There's so many different ways a person can work on a film. It depends on your relationship with the director, and how much of a filmmaker you are, as opposed to being a technician. Often, you are working with a director who wants everything, and for a producer who has nothing, so you end up being the meat in the sandwich.

'I really feel I'm a filmmaker, and I get involved in how a film feels, and what its content and meaning are. But not all sound editors do that. Some of them are just hired guns who come in and cut the sound. I used to do that a bit, and I still do occasionally. My relationship with Noyce is much more intimate than that, and I feel like I own part of his film.'

Because his or her involvement is relatively short — four to five weeks — a mixer who is in demand participates in the making of more feature films than anyone outside of the laboratories. Peter Fenton has mixed around a hundred and fifty of them. This stockpile of knowledge and reminiscences could fill a book of its own, liberally peppered with Fenton's ascerbic wit.

In the making of a film someone of Fenton's experience may be asked their opinion on nearly all matters relating to sound at one time or another. However, his first official appearance is at the screening where decisions are made about post-syncing. Although this phase has already been investigated in the sound editor's segment, some comments from Fenton's perspective are edifying.

'The only time I really see a picture is the first time and the last time. What I mean by "see" is when I can just appreciate the story and the actors, without thinking of it technically at all. I just sit there and think, "Oh, she's terrific", or "That's a bit disappointing."

'The first time I see it, I refuse to have people ask me what to post-sync. At that screening, I get a really good idea of what the picture is about, the feel of the picture. Then I talk to the director, and he might say, "It's very important this guy comes out a hero", even though he doesn't look like a hero to me. But it's very important to get a feeling for what the director feels about his picture.

'After that, you're looking at it purely technically to see what has to be post-sync, which is like learning to play forehand, rather than thinking about the whole game. It's just the one thing.'

Like Greg Bell, Fenton worked on *Echoes of Paradise*, and was influential in the decision to post-sync parts of it. The dialogue in one particularly touching scene was almost being swamped by the roar of the surf, although director Phil Noyce was content because he could still hear the actors.

'It looked like it should be quiet, with little "shhh" waves, rather than the Bondi bloody Lifesaving Club. I talked them into post-syncing some scenes that they didn't want to.

'It's nominated for the AFI awards this year [1987]. I'm not sure it'll win; it's not very loud, and usually the intelligent bloody AFI voters vote for loud soundtracks.

In the event, *Ground Zero* won Best Soundtrack.

Before the final mix begins, the individual tracks — perhaps thirty or forty — will be pre-mixed down to a manageable number. For instance, if there is an exterior scene beside a stream, the soundtrack might include several sounds of running water, a few tracks of birds, some cicadas, and a little wind. These elements could be pre-mixed in relation to each other, and then controlled by a single fader on the desk at the final mix. Pre-mixing is the work of a few days, and is carried out separately by an effects mixer, music mixer and the dialogue mixer, all pre-mixing their individual contributions.

These same three people will be at the desk for the final mix. Occasionally, it may be performed by two or four people, but three is the norm, with the dialogue mixer in charge of proceedings.

'You become like a good tennis doubles team. I can flick into reverse because an effect was too loud, and the effects mixer won't even ask what was wrong with it. He knows.'

The mix takes place in a special mixing theatre, with a huge sound console facing the screen. The mixers work from charts made up by the sound editor which depict all the sounds that have been laid up, which sound tracks they are on, and where they start and end relative to the footage. All the sound tracks are interlocked with the image, so that they can be run forwards, backwards and stopped simultaneously. Brief segments of the film, or specific scenes, are run back and forth, over and over, until the sound is just right: a process known as 'rock and roll'.

In attendance are the director, the sound editor and his crew, often the editor, and sometimes the producer. The sound editor describes his intentions regarding the relationship of the various sound components he has provided. But other people present often wish to have some input also.

'If the director is strong, but is also willing to get ideas from his technicians, there's no problem at all', Fenton commented. 'But it can become aggressive when people are bouncing ideas off each other every minute of the day. It's easy to get a bit of tension, especially if they've been there six hours for one reel. [Ten minutes of film.]

'Mixers generally never object to someone making a suggestion. What's difficult is if four people are all talking at once. What should happen is that the technician should say his piece through the director. There are a couple of directors who insist on it. They won't let anybody else talk to the mixer, which I think is a perfectly good idea.'

This conflict may be more critical when it occurs between the director and the producer. While Fenton runs into this regularly, his solution is straight-forward:

'I work out who I think's the dummy, and who's the bright one, and I go that way. Otherwise I could still be there for a film we did three years ago. I try to go the director's way initially, because I really believe he's got creative control of the picture — it's his go. But if he's off the planet, you're never going to get it done, so you've got to take over. That's part of being a mixer: sometimes you've got to lead.

'We've got a gag about one of our directors in Sydney: if there was a room with two doors, he'd never be in or out...'

The result everyone is trying to achieve is a balance of all sounds in relation to each other. The sounds are unlikely to be moved in relation to the image, with the possible exception of the music, which may be juggled slightly for various effects.

The levels at which different sounds are played are largely determined by the need for realism, but it is also a matter of achieving a desired effect. This is where the mixer's creativity comes into play. Fenton:

'I remember a scene in *The Cars That Ate Paris*, when the cars attack the town. There's a VW with a big spike sticking out of it, on which the baddie's body is impaled. It was all very noisy. John Meillon, the mayor, was talking crazily, the cars were revving, and the blokes were yelling and screaming.

'After a lot of experimentation, we took all of the sound away, and just the music played: a fabulous piece by Bruce Smeaton. Suddenly everyone in the theatre said, "That's it! That's fantastic!" You could have played that scene all sorts of ways; we had so many tracks to run: crowds screaming, motor cars, individual yelling and so on. You could have balanced them in ten different ways.'

Some variations are so slight, a lot of people would not even notice the difference. 'If you took the tape echo off the course announcer in the Melbourne Cup scene from *Phar Lap*, all you'd know is that it's a bit easier to understand his calling of the race: you'd hear the names of the horses more clearly. But with the delay on, it's much more realistic.

'The main thing you need from a director is the realisation that if he's going to experiment, it takes time. And that's fine. Peter Weir always books a long time for his mixes, and he experiments a lot. Sometimes you go over things again and again and again. But he's always receptive, and always appreciative when it's over. You don't get in a situation where someone says , "Oh, for Christ's sake, let's get on with it. We've been here for six hours and we haven't got to two hundred feet yet", which can happen to you, even though they're the ones that have made sure you *haven't* got to two hundred feet yet.

'There is a scene in *High Tide* where the little girl comes into a restaurant with her boyfriend. The other kids are razzing the boyfriend, just because he's got his girlfriend there. These kids are in the background while the stars — Judy Davis and Colin Friels — are talking, and depending on how loudly we played the kids, the scene was different.

'Now it was very important that I knew how Gillian Armstrong felt about the scene. You could have played those kids really low in level, and they would not have been important at all. All your attention would have stayed on Judy and Colin. Or you could play the kids quite loudly, and suddenly you're not so much involved with Judy and Colin; you sort of feel sorry for the boyfriend. You can alter who you're looking at by who you play louder. We mixed the scene a lot of times.

'You're a bit like a musician in that you've got to have the technique to play the instrument, but how good you are depends on what you do with it. I think the aesthetic is more important than the technical thing.'

Mention of music brings us to the other major component of the soundtrack. While the orchestra or band is already pre-mixed, it is still probably divided into three separate tracks for subsequent tampering. For instance, it may become apparent that just the trumpet section is too loud beneath a given stretch of dialogue, so it may be pulled back without dropping the level of the entire orchestra.

'You've got to be careful with music, because even a really good piece can dominate the film if it's too strong. It mightn't be out of balance with the rest of the sound, but it can dominate the image. I think it's really important that the director and the composer be on the one track about music. Too much music in a picture just drives you crazy.'

In an era when stereo predominates, many films are, nonetheless, still cut in mono. Mono pictures will generally be dialogue rather than action oriented, and they require a smaller budget for sound. Mono films include *The Year of Living Dangerously, Bliss, Fringe Dwellers, High Tide,* and *The Place at the Coast.*

Stereo pictures are significantly more complex, because of the potential for sounds to move across the speakers with the image.

'Not all mixers think as I do, but I play all the dialogue in the centre. I just think it can be so confusing if you're sitting in a crook seat in the cinema, and the sound is panning round. If everyone sat in the best seat, you could do it. The exception is when I really want the effect of someone calling out from a long way off screen.'

The third, immensely expensive possibility, is the six-track system commonly used in sci-fi blockbusters, with spaceships screaming through the surround speakers in the cinema.

Whichever system is used, it becomes a classic 'best laid plans' tale: however stunning the mix is, it all comes to nothing if the machinery in the cinema does not play it properly. After a preview of *Les Patterson Saves the World*, Peter Fenton received a panic-stricken phone-call because the sound was apparently dreadful. The next day he went in and found it playing perfectly in one cinema, and abysmally in the next. With a stereo mix, the sound is split between left, centre, right and surround speakers. If the decoding equipment in the cinema is not maintained immaculately, this can all go disastrously haywire.

'The manager of the theatre, another bloody genius, came down and said to me, "We never have any complaints with the American pictures." I said, "Who would you expect to get the complaint from? Fly a few mixers out and see how you go". I mean, to have things sounding great would be for the cinema's benefit, too. It's not just for us.'

Director Gillian Armstrong on location for *High Tide. Photo courtesy of International Film Management Ltd.*

11

Of Vampires and Butterflies

THE DIRECTOR

It may seem that an attempt to illustrate the collaborative nature of filmmaking must, to some extent, undermine the concept of the director as *auteur*. However, a thorough survey of all the consulting, collaborating, and work-sharing that goes into the making of a film reveals the staggering amount of labour a good director logs up. Lesser directors may do less, and their films do not disguise the fact.

Gillian Armstrong, Phillip Noyce and John Duigan are all extremely dedicated directors. To highlight the extent of their collaboration with key members of their support team, the role of director is examined obliquely, via their dealings with these other people. As Gillian Armstrong neatly summed it up, 'The whole point of trying to work with the best people is that you hope they are going to add to your vision; that they will have ideas; that they are going to add layers all the way along.'

It is common for the director to become involved before the final draft of the screenplay is completed. Phil Noyce revelled in the experience of directing four short dramas for Home Box Office television in America, and being provided with an almost complete shooting script.

'That is very rare in Australia, but you live in hope that it will happen. In the case of that project, perhaps it had something to do with the eighty years or more of continuous screenwriting experience that the American cinema now has. I think the hardest part of filmmaking is the scriptwriting process; everything flows from that.

Gillian Armstrong described the birth of *My Brilliant Career*.

'I was approached by the producer Margaret Fink, about the book and then together we chose a scriptwriter. I'd never even heard of the author Miles Franklin, or read the book. *Brilliant Career* was Margaret's baby. She found the book and she was the one who first related to the material and asked me to read it because she thought there was a film there. I also thought there was a film there, but that it would be very expensive and I thought, at that stage, that I was too inexperienced to do it.

However, Armstrong did take on the challenge.

'We had one or two meetings with Eleanor Witcombe, the writer, so that we all agreed about what we actually wanted the film to be, and what we wanted to say.

'Once the producer and director have reached an agreement, a lot of producers I have worked with feel that the director should pass those points on to the writer. Otherwise you can reach a situation — especially when there are two producers — where there are too many people: it gets terribly confusing. A writer can come to a script meeting, and we will all be arguing, and they leave wondering where they're meant to go. I think most producers I've worked with really respect the director's vision. Finally, one person has to hold it all together, and that is the person who has to shoot the thing.

'I spent time with Eleanor just to discuss the approach to adapting the book. We agreed on a number of things that we thought were problems in the book which we hoped the script would solve.

'Knowing that the book was large and that we were going to have to reduce it, we also talked about some ways to do that: one character could go, or a certain part of the plot could go. So those basic things were ironed out, and then she went away and did an outline of how the story would take shape. Then we sat down together with the producer, and talked about the things that were working and not working in the outline.

'There are certain stages where I, as the director, would say to the writer, "Why don't you go away and maybe working through it, you will come up with an answer. Sometimes we don't have to solve it here and now. When you are actually at the typewriter, maybe it will happen". It just depends on the writer, and what they need; how much feedback they want from you. So I would be very involved with them over a year or so.

'I'm like a script editor for the writer. I don't sit there writng lines; I talk about shape, structure, how it is working dramatically, and occasionally, this line or that line, when it gets down to the nitty gritty. But it's more an overall thing. I think it is very important for the writer to have a free hand — the freer the better — because quite often they have better skills.'

High Tide is the only feature film to date with which Armstrong has been involved from the first germ of an idea. When she joined producer Sandra Levy and writer Laura Jones to initiate a then undefined project, she had already considered the possibility of a film based around children looking for their natural parents. Using this idea, the three of them came up with a rough story outline, which Laura Jones took away to write a treatment. She received feedback on this from Gillian and Sandra, and then turned in a first-draft screenplay.

For Phillip Noyce, the scripting stage often involves reworking an existing screenplay himself or with others.

'*Newsfront* was conceived by David Elfick and Philippe Mora before I came to it. They did quite a lot of research on it and came up with an outline. Philippe left the country and Bob Ellis was hired by David Elfick to write a first draft, which I was introduced to a year or a year and a half before we actually started shooting.

'The problem was quite simple. The film was too long and too ambitious in terms of the budget that could be raised under two circumstances: firstly, that it was that type of film, and secondly, that it was within Australia in 1976–77 when the average budget was maybe $400,000. The film was eventually made for $505,000 and it was obvious that the first draft couldn't be made for that, quite apart from the dramatic problems of ebb and flow and focus that were evident in that draft.

'It was a very good script, always, at any draft or at any stage; very well written, with good characters. Bob has a very idiosyncratic way of writing dialogue, and the dialogue was very, very good. Each character was strongly defined by their intonation, the phrases, and the particular words that they used. There is no way I felt equipped to rewrite the dialogue. Rather, I decided what to cut and what to keep, restructured it, and then, through the newsreels, tried to knit the thing together.

'A problem, I think, was that everyone, including Bob, was quite inexperienced in the collaborative process involved in filmmaking. The point about how much money we could raise in this part of the world at that time, to make that sort of film, might not have been clearly communicated to him.

'We only had seven weeks of shooting, and we could never have shot his script in that time. So that script had to be cut. Problems came in obtaining the writer's agreement to cut it, and just what cuts should be made. I think communication broke down for whatever reason — it's ten years ago now, so it's hard to remember everything that happened.

'After I'd done a script edit on Bob's script, I can remember him coming into David's studio at Palm Beach, seeing the typist typing up the new script, and him grabbing the manuscript off the typist's desk, running down Palm Beach Road, and David running out of the studio and tackling him as he raced down the road with the script under his arm, and a hundred and fifty pages just flying off into the air!

'Bob withdrew his name from the film but after it became a success he agreed to be credited. Who's to say whether the original script would have been better? We'll never know. Almost everything that we shot for those seven weeks is in the film — almost every shot! And no day's shooting was finished early, so we couldn't have shot any more than we did.

'Whether we made the right decisions in cutting is also academic at this stage. But it probably would have been better if Bob had embraced the idea that the script needed to be cut for whatever reason, and participated in it right up until the end. That would have been the ideal situation.

'Interestingly enough, there was another version produced for Europe, different to the Australian cut, which cut a further ten minutes out of the film. That won the Best Film of the Year prize from the Belgian Film Critics, and that was a version that was produced against my will, at the insistence of the New South Wales Film Corporation. Even though I reluctantly participated in the production of the short version, I was totally against it, and wrote to the American distributors who were being pressed to distribute that cut, and requested that they insist on the original, which they did.'

At the shooting stage, any rewriting required is undertaken by the writer, if possible; otherwise the director may have a go. Some amendments may arise as a result of the earliest rushes.

'In *Brilliant Career*', recalled Gillian, 'I think Robert Grubb's character [Frank Hawden] was much more charming and funnier than we had envisaged, which was something the actor brought to it. We realised there were a number of scenes where Judy Davis' character [Sybylla] was putting him down, and that was really going to work against her. So we did a few changes there.

'That sort of thing happens during the shoot. Once they are flesh and blood people in their roles, sometimes just the way they come off the screen changes things, and you have to keep an eye on that.

'During the shooting on every film I've worked on except for *Brilliant Career*, the writer has still been involved in the project, and visited the set. They've had a very easy relationship with me, and I discussed the things we were considering cutting. Also, they've often written lines for background scenes — just to help with ad lib stuff.'

Similarly on *Heatwave*, while Phillip Noyce was in the cutting room with John Scott, writer Mark Rosenberg came in and virtually wrote another script for the background and voice-over dialogue that permeates the film.

The process of scripting a film is totally different in all its aspects when the director is also the writer, which is not uncommon in Australia. John Duigan is a notable example:

'If I was offered a script I really liked, I would certainly do it. But as I am primarily involved in film as a way of exploring ideas, it is more likely that the particular ideas that interest me at any particular time are the ones that I'll come up with myself, and write a script about. But I'm always on the lookout for other scripts, and I do get sent quite a lot.

'In the best collaborations between writers and directors, you have a script with a singular vision which the director, coming from quite a different perspective, can crystallise and sometimes enlarge upon. But it is quite rare that a writer seems completely satisfied with the way their script is handled by a director, so often collaborations between writers and directors seem to be fairly spikey.

'There are potential advantages and disadvantages to the writer/director situation. There is, perhaps, a risk of a lack of objectivity. On the other hand there is likely to be a strong sense of unity between the text and its interpretation in its final filmic form. Obviously the writer/director needs to be receptive to the input of his or her collaborators. You get a lot of inspiration and expansion of your ideas from working with the actors and the key crew.'

The producer can be a vital creative partner for the director. Even a director such as Duigan who initiates all his own projects, is fundamentally reliant on the producer:

'They have to see the potential of an idea in order to agree to produce it and to raise the money for it.'

'I want to know everything about a producer right from the very beginning', declared Gillian Armstrong. 'I won't work with a producer unless I feel that we have the same sensibilities; that they see casting the same way; that ultimately they see the integrity of the story as the most important thing of all, and not the so-called commerciality of the story.

'It is such an important relationship that I have actually turned down scripts I really liked because I haven't wanted to work with the producer attached to them. I know that the time when the producer/director relationship doesn't work out is when those essential ingredients aren't there from the beginning: that ultimately they don't want to make the same film that you want to make — they don't have the same concerns. They think that there are artificial things that will make a film successful, such as some box-office star, or some American name, or some hip tune. So I'm extremely tentative in setting up a relationship with a new producer. Partly I assess them by the quality of the films that they have made before, and also their reasons for making the film that they come to me with. The element of taste is pretty hard to set up as a test — it's not just what colour shirt they are wearing. Things like the cast, the music and the titles will just be battles unless they have some sensitivity to the way that you see things. Or else you totally protect yourself, in your contract, and have control over all that area.'

Phillip Noyce reached into a filing cabinet, and pulled out a contract from which to quote on his degree of autonomy: his right of approval regarding script, cast, music, locations, sets and principal crew. To our mutual surprise and amusement, he read out the following:

'The production company will seriously consider the director's views on the above matters. The production company shall have the sole and exclusive right to make any and all decisions in relation to all matters pertaining to the film.'

This was followed by an expletive and laughter. Mr Noyce was going to investigate the matter...

'Most director's contracts usually give you the right to choose those people', he maintained. 'I've never had a case where I've had to work with anyone I didn't really want to work with. But, on the other hand, I have had cases where I haven't got my first choice, necessarily. A producer would be silly to put a director with someone that they've said they can't work with, or they don't want to work with. That would be suicidal.

'In an ideal world, you work very closely with your producer and you constantly use him as one of the essential sounding boards. As a director, you always look for steadfast collaborators. Steadfast in as much as they won't follow the strongest voice, or the person who seems to be most committed about something. They should have an original opinion, whether it is based on a genuine understanding of the principles of drama, or a genuine understanding of audience response. But not so steadfast that they won't be able to change an opinion if something presents itself that is genuinely better.

'The producer often understands the origins of the whole project: the concept, the ideals, and all of the fantasies people have when they go into making a movie. And it is always good to hold on to those, as all these other people come in for lesser or greater periods, and make individual contributions to the film.'

In this country producers choose directors more often than directors choose their producers, so it would seem that a producer is 'casting' the right director to some degree. Gillian Armstrong:

'I think I've done enough films now that they should be able to judge what they'll get from me. I know with *Starstruck* I went to David Elfick and said that I wanted to do it. He didn't say to my face, "She makes boring period pictures", but it was after *Brilliant Career*, and obviously that is what everyone thought — sort of lace and soft lighting. He started that relationship a little bit worried about me, and how much I really knew about rock music, and all that sort of stuff.

'We didn't always see eye to eye about casting, either. At the beginning, I think he felt we needed names for *Starstruck*. But ultimately, when we found Ross O'Donovan and Jo Kennedy, he thought they were wonderful and has been like a father figure to them ever since.

'Margaret Fink and I got on very well. We have very similar tastes. During casting for *Brilliant Career* I put people down on video and she came and looked at them at the end of the day. I'd get home and think, "No, no, that person is *wrong*". I'd be just about to dial her number when she'd ring me and say, "I've been thinking about that person..." It was a great rapport.

'On *Mrs Soffel*, it was a big battle to get Mel Gibson. The studio didn't want us to get a name. They thought Diane Keaton was enough. Normally, it is the other way round and they want everyone to be a star. We actually had a star who wanted to be in it, and the studio was trying to talk me into someone who'd be cheaper. But the producers backed me on the decision. I screen-tested a lot of other leading men and they agreed he was the best.

'With *High Tide*, the whole idea was to try and keep the budget as small as possible. We were going to make it with no names at all, and Sandra Levy went out to raise the money on that basis. She managed to get a pre-sale on the script and me.'

At that stage, the central character was a man, which the writer, director and producer finally agreed should be changed to a woman instead.

'I really could not think of anyone better than Judy Davis. Both the choice of Judy in *High Tide* and Mel in *Mrs Soffel* were choices about an actor, not a name. So we actually had to go back to the distributors, Hemdale, and say, "The good news is we've got Judy Davis — you have a name. But the bad news is we need more money". (In fact, the Australian Film Commission came up with the extra money, not Hemdale.)

'Sandra was totally supportive in all the casting. We were together when Claudia Karvan came to one of the very early sessions, were totally struck by her, and thought when she walked out the door that she was Ally. I was the one who said, "Yes, she's fantastic, but I still feel that I should see another two hundred girls first, because she is only the fourth we have seen". And Sandra supported me in that.

'All of my producers have been on location. Although Margaret Fink was in Sydney some of the time, she still saw rushes and would ring me. You want to know what they think the performances are like, what the lighting is like, and whether they are getting a sense of how the scene is working. Basically, on location you just want them to tell you that it's all wonderful...'

Gillian Armstrong prefers all money matters to be out in the open between director and producer, and said she feels a responsibility in relation to her budget. It came as a bombshell on *Brilliant Career* when she was told that the art department was somewhere near $20,000 over budget, a fact which had remained hidden from the scrutiny of even the producer.

'I was told that I couldn't have any wind machines to create the dust storm in the opening scene. That's the sort of thing that people are probably unaware of. They think the directors just go out and talk to actors, and point the camera at sunsets and dawns, and make the movie. But all the time you are worrying about the economics of the situation: trying to get the best on the screen, and trying to balance things.

'When that happened on *Brilliant Career*, I went to Margaret and said, "Help! This is the opening scene of the film. How am I going to shoot it with one fan?" That was all they could fly to Hay. She just had to say, "Oh, I'm sorry kid. The money's gone". But through the collaboration of the first assistant Mark Egerton, the director of photography Don McAlpine, and myself — worrying and working and trying to have inspiration at night — we finally came up with a way to shoot the opening sequence with only one fan. Then I worked out the idea of shooting the dust storm from inside the house, through the window, so we only had to cover the frame of the window with dust, rather than having to cover the whole landscape.

'Mark and the art department worked out the logistics of throwing dust across the window for the length of the dialogue. They were a fantastic crew, all out there — Make-up, Wardrobe, everyone — throwing dirt across the screen. Don McAlpine did a wheelie in one of the crew vehicles and zipped out of frame, and that was the dust in front of the house in the opening wide-shot.

'For any director, your team is so important, because so many times they can help solve things in a practical sense. That is the real joy of filmmaking, when you feel that they are all running around for the sake of the film. And the *Brilliant Career* episode was one instance where, ultimately, I think it was an inspiration. It was better for the story that we were inside with Sybylla, and this world was happening outside that we were not a part of, and she was not a part of — she was cut off.'

While that problem emanated specifically from the art department, the day-to-day money worries are the domain of the production manager. Phillip Noyce:

'In my experience, the best films have resulted from a situation where the production manager tries to get inside your head. Probably not because your ideas are any better, but because finally, when the shit hits the fan, it is much better that everyone has a unified idea. In an ideal world, they are making decisions on your behalf, having learnt what your priorities are.'

John Duigan observed that the production manager should be able to make all sorts of logistical decisions and compromises that the director need not even know about. This suits Duigan perfectly, as long as he is warned of problems and advised of changes.

'For me, the proof of the efficiency of the production manager is when I don't get any surprises: people are there on set when they are called, and they are not complaining about the size of their room or that the plumbing has gone off or that there are no toilets available, or whatever.

'If the DOP has said that they need an arc light for five nights, and the production is really stretched, the production manager will come to me and say, "Do you really need it? If you do, we can probably juggle things around, and you can have it". It might come down to having a cherry picker on one night at the expense of cutting a few extras on another. In those situations, having agreed to work within a particular budget, I try and go along with the necessary compromises that are there. I think there are some directors who would choose not to compromise, and there are good arguments why they shouldn't, for the creative veracity of what it is they are doing.

'Because I come from a background of low-budget filmmaking, I do actually take quite an interest in the evolution of the budget, and try to be aware of how things are going financially. I get a copy of the daily production report sent to me each day so that I am in touch with things like ratio, and whether we've achieved everything that we wanted to, and what sort of problems have occurred.

'But when films run successfully, there's not a huge amount of liaison that I have with the production manager. Generally, they'll just ask me if there are any problems, and I'll tell them it went very well, and that's it.'

On *High Tide*, associate producer Greg Ricketson overlapped his role with that of the first-time production manager, Julie Forster. Armstrong:

'We knew one of the biggest expenses on *High Tide* would be putting the crew up on location. Whether or not to shoot on location was something Sandra Levy, Greg and I discussed. We decided that it was very much a story about a place, and that it was an isolated place, so it wasn't going to work in Maroubra or Botany or Newcastle.

'First we talked about whether to shoot it in Sydney, so we wouldn't have to pay for everyone's accommodation. When we couldn't find anywhere in Sydney, the next option was to shoot it somewhere close to Sydney, because it was going to save so much in bringing actors back and forth. Ultimately, we decided as a team — basically my decision with their support — that it was worth the extra expense to go to Merimbula (on the south coast of NSW).

'Then we went through it to see how much money would be saved if we brought some scenes back to Sydney, and which scenes they could be. The first assistant would be involved in this, because someone can make a decision off the top of their head that they think it might be cheaper to shoot the caravan interiors in Sydney, but then the first assistant will say, "But I've got no weather cover down there, so in the end it might work out much more expensive when we need some interiors down on location". So Mark Turnbull, the First, was also involved in those discussions.

'I was involved because there were certain scenes I wanted to be in emotional order; that for the sake of the performers, I didn't want to put totally out of order. So all those things were considered.

'After the producer and the DOP, the First, for me, is the most important person in my entire crew. I've been very lucky that I've worked with such fantastic Firsts in this country. They help a director to get the best on the screen in every possible way. They help you have the camera in the place you want it, at the right time to get the best light. They help you with a schedule which is helping your actors and their whole emotional growth toward the character and the role. If they are good Firsts, they make sure you get the most important shots done in a day — the shots that are the key to your whole film.

'Having worked in Canada and the USA, I realise how lucky we are. The Firsts here are much better trained to try and get the best quality on the screen for the least amount of money. And the mood that the actors are in when they arrive on set, when I have to try and help them to get a performance, is very much to do with the First's team: how they relate to actors, and how they look after them.

'Also, my Firsts have been involved in decisions about script edits, too. I've always worked with very intelligent, perceptive people, who have often been the clear voice of reason when we're sitting around wondering what to cut, because we're two days over. They are the ones who have often said something like, "Don't you think it was a bit pointless seeing her walk into the house?". I feel very lucky that I've had that intelligence in my Firsts, as well as a creative understanding of the script.'

Most directors go through the schedule with the First to confirm that enough time has been allotted for shooting each scene. John Duigan:

'Fairly early on in the piece, they would need to get some understanding about how you plan to do a scene. There might be a scene which looks fairly simple in the script, but in which you have decided that you want to have a particularly elaborate shot. In discussions on the schedule, those sorts of things emerge.

'On the set, there are a lot of very difficult judgements a first assistant has to make, like whether to start hassling a director about hurrying up within a scene, simply because by spending a lot of time on one scene, it means that the next scene is going to have to be done in, say, a master shot alone. The First has to really get to know the director he is working with to know whether he can trust the decisions of the director, and whether or not to fight those decisions.

'The First needs to judge whether the director is tired, or losing objectivity, or has a heavy cold, or whatever, and can come in and say, "Look, I really think you should move on at this stage". In a situation where you are losing light, and the day is becoming very urgent, a First may sometimes suggest a way of simplifying a series of set-ups. I'll certainly listen to what they have to say, and sometimes I might take up their ideas.'

There is a period during pre-production, after the script and finances are settled, and usually before casting is complete, when the art department is of paramount importance to the director. Duigan:

'In the initial discussions with the production designer, one suggests a framework in which the film is to operate. That can be fairly detailed, but it can still give an enormous amount of room to move for the designer. We may talk about the nature of the script and what we are attempting to achieve with it; perhaps a colour range that we choose to operate in. I might bring along a series of colours and other materials that I feel are appropriate, to use as a basis for discussion. The production designer will probably have a whole lot of ideas of his or her own, and out of a synthesis of the ideas that both of us have, the look of the film will take shape.

'With some projects, I probably have a more pronounced vision of a style than in others. The longer I work in film, the more strongly I think about that side of the film beforehand. The selection of a production designer will, in part, be made on how they respond to the concepts that I have for a film.

'The allegorical nature of *One Night Stand*, for example, was there in the script. The mechanical doll, the rabbit, the characters from *Alice in Wonderland*, and all that kind of thing was scripted, but even within these dictates, a production designer, responding and liking the ideas that are there, still has a lot of scope to bring his own vision to the project. There is a constant dialogue in the pre-production period. I would like to think that even though I've got a strong concept, it is essentially a starting point, and I think a lot of designers probably like to have that, so that they know they are going to be working in a way which is in sync with the director's view.

'But even a detailed starting point still gives an enormous amount of room to move. If you say, as far as the costumes are concerned, that you want to dress the artists up in the sort of stylish, long, silhouette looks of the late 1920s, that is not really being very specific. I don't know enough about the materials that exist in costume to spell out exactly what I want, but I can bring together a few adjectives and say approximately what would be good ideas to look for. Often the designer will bounce off that, and come up with a slight variation that will be an improvement on what I'd thought. Certainly this has often been the case in my experience of working with people like Roger Ford, Ross Major, Lee Whitmore etc.

'In the case of *Newsfront*', said Phillip Noyce, 'there wasn't a strong design concept expressed within the screenplay, but we were working from a marriage of fictional materials and newsreels and the characters had to be dressed authentically. We also had the problem of some sections being in black and white, and some in colour.

'The more subtle design concepts came from discussions on how I was going to interpret the screenplay. If you remember the film, it is divided into chapters, separated by a photograph of one or two of the characters from the next section, with a date caption. The design decisions evolved from my explanation of what each section was about: how we were interpreting it and what we were going for historically and within the fictional story, because of the constant interplay between the two.

'The principal design choice is the choice of the people that you work with, really. Once you get Brian Thomson to design your picture, you know you are going to get a certain look, and if you get Wendy Dickson to design it, you're going to get another look. So in choosing people, you are committing yourself, in the same way as a producer is when choosing a director. They are committing themselves to a certain type of film, with certain preoccupations: emphases made in particular directions at the expense of others.

'The main thing in working with a designer is that you are hoping they come up with more ideas than you could have come up with; that they extend your own vision. Otherwise, what is the use of having them? But it is very important they don't submerge the director's interpretation, otherwise the film is going to go off in so many directions that it won't make any sense.

'With every department, you go into as much detail as you possibly can in the time that you have. In the case of design, that means every set, every costume, every car. But it doesn't always work out like that. Except where a designer's ideas are absolutely offensive, you will tend to go with them, on the principle that you have already made the decision to choose them, so it is your responsibility to respond to their ideas. But I certainly wouldn't see it as some sort of struggle for supremacy of vision. The only struggle you have is to make a better film, and interpret the drama in a way that is going to communicate something to the audience.'

Gillian Armstrong said that over the years she has learned to ensure that any strong images conjured up by a script are passed on to the designer.

'I remember on *Brilliant Career*, with Luciana Arrighi, an absolutely wonderful designer, I always had an image of a picket fence in front of the house in the drought. I'd seen a lot of stills of that sort of pathetic attempt at gentility in the 1890s in the middle of the bush. When I got to Hay, the art department had created this very rustic sort of farm fence, and I remember I was very disappointed about that. But I got back the next morning, and there was a picket fence! I don't know what they did. They raided the graveyard or something, I think.'

The third major voice in determining the visual style of a picture is the director of photography. John Duigan:

'We discuss the shooting style that I have in mind for the film, the overall emotional feel, and the way the look and the lighting can contribute to that. During that discussion, we probably refer to other films as examples of what we are talking about.

'We might test different film stocks. For example, we used Agfa stock for the daylight scenes in *The Year My Voice Broke*, whereas we used Kodak for the night exterior scenes. We discuss the look of particular actors when we do the tests on the actors, and sometimes examine them from particular angles. At that stage, we will also have discussions with Make-up. Then each evening at rushes we sit together and quietly discuss individual shots as we go through, and generally take stock of how uniform the look that we're achieving is. The proof of the pudding is seeing the rushes, when I will either say, "Yes, that's exactly what we were after", or, "No, it didn't quite work", or whatever. It is unusual for us to disagree over whether something is right or wrong, but it occasionally does happen.

'I know I have a particular dislike for extremely low lighting, which is a very fashionable way of lighting these days. There was an example on *The Year My Voice Broke*, where I felt that a shot was too dark because I couldn't see the change of expression on a face clearly enough. Geoff Burton, the DOP, disagreed, and liked it like that. We did redo the shot in question, and he put up what he called a "Duigan Light" to achieve what I wanted. He gave me an article to read by Nestor Almendros, a cinematographer working in America, in which Nestor explains about a similar experience that he had with a director. Geoff was thinking of sending him his definition of the Duigan Light, so that Nestor could use it on occasions as required...

'*The Year My Voice Broke* is fairly strongly realist in its look, but in subtle ways there are colourings that are used both to beautify certain things, and to attempt to convey the sense of mystery in the conception of the world that the principal characters of Danny and Freya have. This works very well for a lot of the scenes, where we used day-for-night which comes across with a slightly ethereal, bluish quality that I like very much, such as the cemetery scene, where Danny [Noah Taylor] finds Freya [Loene Carmen] miscarrying, and runs up the hill. It was Geoff's idea to do day-for-night — he saw the possibility of using it for the purposes that I've described.

'*Winter of Our Dreams* is an urban picture, which contrasts two distinct realities: that of the Judy Davis character — a junkie working on the streets of Kings Cross — and the slightly sterile world of two middle-class idealists, who have become jaded. So there is a difference between those two worlds that Tom Cowan and I attempted to complement with the lighting and the shooting styles.

'In Judy's world, there are generally more shots, and a slightly faster editing pattern, slightly more jarring angles, and a grittier look in the lighting of it. The world of Cathy Downes' and Bryan Brown's place has a more graceful, languid sort of quality, with more master shots and more and slower tracks, and a slightly more sterile look in the lighting.

'*One Night Stand* is a sort of allegory about naivety, in many ways: the naivety of the characters in it, and through them, of the society as a whole. That is expressed in part by what could be called a shallower lighting look. There is a clarity in the contrasts in *One Night Stand*, and far more use of primary colours that are sometimes quite over the top and theatrical. There is a heightened reality, a slightly expressionistic reality, and so, accordingly, there isn't the same attempt at realism that there is in *Winter.*'

In much the same way as a total visual style is developed in collaboration with the DOP, an aural style may be developed with the sound recordist. Gillian Armstrong put this to good effect on *High Tide*:

'I talked to Ben Osmo about how it would be great to use different surfs and so on, almost as a musical score, so he spent a lot of time getting us wonderful water sounds. An example of input on the more practical side was making the caravans not sound like boxes, which also involved the art department. The caravans were designed with the sound department in mind.'

John Duigan relies on the recordist to help monitor the consistency of performance in relation to sound levels.

'They can also keep you in touch with things like variations in accent, or some aspect of a person's diction that worries me, or the propensity for sibilance in somebody's voice.

'The relationship between the boom swinger and the actors is quite important, because it is potentially irritating to the actors to constantly have someone reaching up their dress to put a microphone on their midriff, or whatever, so the boom swinger has to be pretty sensitive.

'After a take, a good sound recordist will come and say, "I couldn't really understand what that line meant", and I'll go and listen and make a decision about it. They will also listen to performance, and if they think a performance is down, or if someone is speaking as if they have a hangover, they quietly let you know that, which is another kind of important information that is coming to you.'

The continuity person also monitors performances, and provides further insurance that the director is getting what he needs from the actors. Duigan:

'There are occasions when they have seen a moment in rehearsal which perhaps has been forgotten, or isn't quite being struck, so they say, "Remember in the rehearsal, you liked the way he just took a little glance out of the corner of his eye, to show that he actually picked up on what she was doing", or something like that. They are invaluable for that. Also, the best continuity people will express opinions about things that they feel don't ring true, or seem inconsistent.

'But it is very easy, as a director, to be brusque with your continuity person. It is unfortunately one of the burdens that Continuity has to bear. I'm aware that sometimes I give them a bit of a hard time. It usually is a product of the pace you have to shoot at on low-budget films, and the last thing you feel you want is someone saying, "But you didn't quite get that, that time". However, often what they have to say is important, and I try and act on it, in spite of my initial impulses or irritation.'

'The DOP, the Continuity, the First — the people who are closest to the director while they're actually shooting — all have lots of suggestions all the time,' said Gillian Armstrong. 'Most of the people I've worked with have been fantastic. I've been very lucky. I could ask any of them what they thought, if I wanted to. I don't stand there having great committee meetings, but it is certainly nice to know that they are there at times, such as if I've had the producer tell me I'm selecting too many print-takes, and I've got to start cutting down. That is when Continuity can be helpful, because quite often, if you've done a few takes, you start to lose track of them. Continuity will say, "Are you sure you want four *and* five, because they are very close?" "Yeah, I suppose you're right..." It's a very close relationship.

'I've found that a lot of people in Continuity are dedicated to the script. They know it, and the story, so often you get wonderful feedback from them. There are times when you are so swamped by the practicalities of the set, it is wonderful that there is someone there who is really looking after the script, and reminding you of things like, "Hey, don't forget that character is going to say *that* later on". They are really the writer's best friend; they're the ones that are looking after the baby.

'Also, I'm totally reliant on Continuity to worry about crossing-the-line. All my films are story-boarded, but when they move the furniture, and we all get upside down on the floor with some camera angle, then Continuity and the DOP can argue that one out. I've never been interested.'

As the absent partner in the process, the editor has to make the best of whatever the director and the crew have provided. This distance from the day-to-day bunfight on set furnishes the editor with an objectivity towards the material which all directors rely on.

'On a dreadful day', said Armstrong, 'when a lot of things go wrong, you can feel like what you shot is a disaster. But the editor is removed from what happened on the day. I think it is great that the editor is not there on the set, and doesn't see the things that are out of frame, like the dust storm in *Brilliant Career*. They just look at it and say, "Yeah, that looks like a dust storm to me". They don't know that you had Wardrobe and Make-up and everyone throwing handfuls of dust in the air. It is very important that they are like your audience. They're just judging what is on celluloid.

'Nick Beauman is extremely good at storytelling and giving suggestions about moving or cutting scenes. We often change the structure in post-production.

'There was a sub-plot in *High Tide* in which the little boy that Claudia has a relationship with went off and joined some Christians. We felt that the relationship between Judy and Claudia was so strong that it was all the audience really wanted to see, and the sub-plot was slowing it down. Nick and I have worked together for so long, and have been through this so many times before, that the first time we saw *High Tide*, he said, "You know and I know that it's not working, and it's slowing down the story. Let's get rid of it".

'I rang Sandra Levy and said, "We've looked at it, and I think there's about twenty minutes that should go. I want you to see it before we take it out, because it's such a lot". We had talked about cutting it before we started shooting, but Laura Jones, the writer, was very strong about it. When Laura saw an early cut, she said, "Well, yeah the Christians went," and we all talked about how we wished we had cut them out before shooting.

'Generally, I wouldn't show a writer the very first cut. I think they'd be too depressed. It's not that they should be depressed about their work, but that they'd be depressed about what I'd done to their work.

'First cuts are generally terrible for everybody, and I often like to see them before the producer does, so I can really steel myself and at least have time to think about it. Then I can say to the producer, and everyone who is crawling out of the screening, "It's alright! We can save it!"

'I'm sensitive enough that, like anyone, I hate people telling me what I already know. I see a film, and I know the opening is too slow or whatever; it finishes, the lights come on, and the producer says, "that opening is too slow", and you reply, with gritted teeth, "I know it is".

Each night at rushes during a shoot, Duigan seeks feedback from the editor about the quality and consistency of performances. When the shoot is over, he lets the editor assemble an initial rough-cut, after indicating the takes that he wants to use.

'I shoot every scene for a particular cut, and the editor's cut will usually be an approximation of that. Occasionally, it might be a radical departure from that, which sometimes might be good, and sometimes I might not like it. But to allow the editor that cut can be a good way of distancing yourself from the material a bit. Also, it allows them to make a very distinctive creative contribution to the way the material is treated. After that point, I work with them fairly solidly to the end of the fine cut.'

Duigan likes the producer to keep a creative distance from the project until the latter stages of post-production, to contribute fresh objectivity.

'Filming the material, and supervising the editing, you can sometimes become very close to it, and want to cuddle a scene and keep it in when it doesn't deserve its place. An important dialogue can occur between the producer and the director at that stage, and very good, experienced producers can fulfil that role.'

Phillip Noyce observed that the relationship between himself and an editor is one that evolves as their objectivity waxes and wanes.

'By the end of the shoot, the director is barely able to stand up, but the editor is quite okay. As you get further and further towards the fine cut, the editor is working longer and longer hours. You might have a discussion for five minutes that takes the editor five hours to put into effect, while the director is just sitting around, smoking cigarettes, or lying on the couch.'

'As you get further in, the editor gets more and more fatigued, so I find that, towards the end, you really need to have your wits about you, although you can't rely totally on yourself either. The producer often becomes an unreliable witness because they have seen every cut, and the outsiders you sometimes invite to screenings can't compensate for the lack of music or the lack of opticals; that is, the incomplete nature of a rough cut screening.

'It is often the sound editing crew and the composer who will be the most reliable people, because they are experienced enough to know what is possible, having seen fifty films at varying stages, before. They can compensate for technical deficiencies that will be overcome later.

'It might be that you pick the brains of the second assistant sound editor after a screening: "Let's have a talk. What did you think of that? What's your overall feeling? Did you find it was too slow? Too fast? How did you feel about that character? Were you scared? Did you like that person? Did you find that person too haughty? Did you see any change in this person throughout the film?" Stuff like that. The second assistant sound editor might be an ideal person in that situation, because they might be young — therefore closer to the mean audience — and yet they have a technical knowledge that enables them to participate in a discussion about the film at that stage.'

Phillip Noyce has a reputation as a director with a special empathy for sound:

'All I can say about sound is that I'm a great believer in the two percent theory. That is, in all scenes in all films, everyone is trying to make everything two percent better. It all comes back to this thing of trying to draw as much as you can out of people. It so happens that sound is your last opportunity. By that stage, I am usually desperate for another two percent, because the picture is locked off. You are not going to change the image, but you've still got the sound, and you'll work it over and over as much as you can, just for another two percent.

'In my experience, it is often that two percent that can make the difference to a picture. After the first cut of *Newsfront* I was catatonic for two days. It was a complete mess. The process of trying to give order to all of that was just a thousand two percents here and there. You change a close-up on an actor, and it can swing the whole performance. You change the intonation of an actor in post-sync dialogue for a key scene, and they can go from an average performance to winning an AFI award.

'So sound comes last, and I just try and exploit it, because there is nothing else that you can work with. You hope that your dubbing editor will take the film places that you couldn't take it. Through the new vision and extended interpretation they provide, you hope it will take a quantum leap.

'After a screening of *Dead Calm*, I said to one of the sound effects editors, "When he swings into the bottom of the boat, what did you think he was doing?" He replied, "I thought he was testing to see whether the boat was leaking, but I thought that not everyone would know that, so I've got an idea for a particular sound when he sticks the knife in the bottom of the boat". He was on exactly the same wavelength as I was.'

'On *The Year My Voice Broke*', said John Duigan, 'we were adding a sense of foreboding — elements of the mystical — to the realism. I gave the sound editors my notes on the sort of effects we might have and what we would attempt to achieve with the soundtrack.

'There was a quite detailed discussion on the role of the dogs in the soundtrack. About once a week during the track-laying period, I'd have a listen to some of the special effects. The dog howl effects were quite hard to get, and went through several permutations. We were listening to different kinds of dogs, dingoes, wolves, hyenas, and various other beasts. It is obviously pretty interesting for the dubbing editors to be hunting out something which is as important as that in the final product.'

Simultaneously, as the sound editor works, the composer creates the score. This is one area where it is practically impossible for the director to keep a day-to-day eye on developments. Gillian Armstrong:

'I talk to them about the style and the emotional needs of the music. I tell them I'm not trained musically, but that I will be able to tell instinctively from my emotional reactions to the music whether I feel it works. I like to hear demos early on, and composers have been great in letting me hear lots of stuff. I think they have felt that the only way to communicate with a moron like me is to actually play it, and I'll say something like, "Yeah, but that feels a bit down. It needs to feel happier". That is the way I would express it.

'On *Mrs Soffel*, knowing that it was a very dramatic film, and a deeply romantic film, I wanted a composer who hadn't worked in that area, because I thought if the score was too 'on the nose', that it would send up the film. Nick Beauman is very good with music, and he always comes with me to the sessions with the composer. It was Nick who put Sybylla's piano playing at the end of *Brilliant Career* at the first screening, and it just worked wonderfully.'

'With the composer you are very careful about what you say', explained Noyce. 'Probably more so even than with the actors. The briefing session might last a week, sitting at the editing bench, going over and over a scene, making sure that the information that you give is exactly what you want. The reason is that you won't see it until it is finished. You'll have almost no further input. If it is an orchestral score, there is no way you are going to get a thirty piece orchestra in to do a demo to show what it is going to be like. And there is usually no way that a single instrument can ever indicate what it is like.'

By contrast, John Duigan finds it useful for the composer to provide rough sketches of the music before it is fully developed, and has even had composers ring him up and play a melody through the telephone.

With the music recorded and all the soundtracks laid up, the sound mix is generally the director's last opportunity to have a significant effect on the way the film finishes up. Duigan likened the relationship between the sound mixer and himself to that between an editor and a director:

'It is a collaboration in which you give an overall description of what you are attempting to achieve with the soundtrack, and then you sit there side-by-side, and they play you permutations, to which you say, "Yes", or "More of this", or whatever. During that process, they sometimes come up with concepts for particular scenes that hadn't occurred to you.'

'They have a technical knowledge which you are dependent on', said Noyce. 'Will this word be heard in the cinema? Will the surround sound really come through? And so on. In addition, they have a whole box of tricks that they have picked up from experience, particularly when you are dealing with stereo.

'But for overall interpretation of the sound, they are dependent on the principal sound editor to reveal what is there and how it might be used, and on the director for guidance. However, like everyone, you hope the sound mixer reveals something that you could never imagine if he wasn't there, whether it is technical or creative — the two go hand in hand at that stage.'

At the end of it all, the director presents the producer with a finished product. Gillian Armstrong:

'After you've spent two years of your life on something, you don't like to see it being sold in a way that denegrates the project. *High Tide* had the only poster that has gone out that I didn't want my name on. Because of a weakness in the producer's contract with the distributor, the distributor designed the poster — a mistake neither Sandra nor I will make again. They overruled us on the TV ad as well.'

Armstrong normally has the right to approve posters as part of her contract with the producer.

'In my experience', commented Phillip Noyce, 'most producers consult you on all those sorts of things, if for no other reason than you might have a better idea than they have. The same with distributors: individual distributors consult you on poster design, press kit content, stills selection, trailers and television commercials, because you might have a better idea, or *one more idea*, which is the most precious thing.

'In making a film, the director has to be not only like a vampire, and suck everyone dry of ideas, but also like a butterfly collector. That is, you go out into a field where there are a million butterflies, or ideas, floating around. You try and catch as many as you can, but there are always nine hundred and ninety thousand that you don't catch. Of the fifty people who work on the film, there are usually forty of them who have a good idea that day, but somehow you can't fit it on the screen. That will always happen.'

Biographies

(The films included are a selection only.)

ANDREWS, Steve, b. Narromine, NSW, 1953. Films as first assistant director include: *Stanley, Mad Max: Beyond Thunderdome, Bodyline* (mini-series), *The Dismissal* (mini-series), *Evil Angels.*

ARMSTRONG, Gillian, b. Melbourne, Vic, 1950. Films as director include: *The Singer and the Dancer, My Brilliant Career, Starstruck, Mrs Soffel, High Tide.*

BARNARD, Antonia, b. England, 1949. Films as production manager include: *Stanley, Mad Max: Beyond Thunderdome, Bodyline* (mini-series), *Echoes of Paradise.*

BEAUMAN, Nick, b. England, 1940. Films as editor include: *My Brilliant Career, Mrs Soffel, Twelfth Night, The Place at the Coast, High Tide.*

BELL, Greg, b. Sydney, NSW, 1951. Films as sound editor include: *Sunday Too Far Away, Picnic at Hanging Rock, My Brilliant Career, Newsfront, Gallipoli.*

BOYD, Russell, b. Melbourne, Vic, 1944. Films as director of photography include: *Picnic at Hanging Rock, Gallipoli, Phar Lap, Crocodile Dundee.*

BUCKLEY, Tony, b. Sydney, NSW, 1937. Films as producer include: *Caddie, The Irishman, The Killing of Angel Street, Kitty and the Bagman, Bliss.*

BUTTERWORTH, Syd, b. Sydney, NSW, 1932. Films as sound recordist include: *Running on Empty, Careful He Might Hear You, Burke and Wills, Travelling North.*

CARROLL, Matt, b Coolah, NSW, 1944. Films as producer include: *Sunday Too Far Away, Stormboy, The Club, Breaker Morant, Freedom.*

COPPING, David, b. England, 1936. Films as production designer include: *The Cars That Ate Paris, Picnic at Hanging Rock, The Picture Show Man, Breaker Morant, Puberty Blues, Fields of Fire* (mini-series).

DE ROCHE, Everett, b. USA, 1946. Films as writer include: *Long Weekend, Patrick, Harlequin, Razorback, Fortress.*

DUIGAN, John, b. England, 1949. Films as director include: *Winter of Our Dreams, Far East, One Night Stand, The Year My Voice Broke.*

EGERTON, Mark, b. England, 1948. Films as first assistant director include: *Picnic at Hanging Rock, My Brilliant Career, Gallipoli, Mosquito Coast.*

FENTON, Peter, b. Boggabri, NSW, 1936. Films as mixer include: *Gallipoli, Phar Lap, Bliss, Burke and Wills, The Fringe Dwellers, High Tide.*

FLETCHER, Colin, b. Sydney, NSW, 1948. Films as first assistant director include: *Careful He Might Hear You, The Coolangatta Gold, The Empty Beach, Travelling North.*

JAMES, Peter, b. Sydney, NSW, 1947. Films as director of photography include: *Caddie, The Irishman, Rebel, The Right Hand Man, The Wild Duck.*

LEWIS, Mark, b. Penrith, NSW, 1952. Films as sound recordist include: *Monkey Grip, The Coca-Cola Kid, Silver City, Rebel, Wind Rider.*

NOYCE, Phillip, b. Griffith, NSW, 1950. Films as director include: *Newsfront, Heatwave, Backroads, Echoes of Paradise, Dead Calm.*

QUIGLEY, Jenny, b. Sydney, 1946. Films as continuity person include: *The Pirate Movie, Brothers, Eureka Stockade* (mini-series), *Dead Calm.*

RICKETSON, Greg, b. Melbourne, Vic, 1954. Films as production manager include; *Puberty Blues, Dead Easy, Careful He Might Hear You, The More Things Change.*

SCOTT, Jane, b. England, 1945. Films as producer include: *Goodbye Paradise, Crocodile Dundee* (as line producer), *Echoes of Paradise, Crocodile Dundee II.*

SCOTT, John, b. Burnie, Tas, 1944. Films as editor include: *The Adventures of Barry McKenzie, Newsfront, Heatwave, One Night Stand, Roxanne.*

WALKER, Grace, b. Sydney, NSW, 1943. Films as production designer include: *Mad Max II, Mad Max: Beyond Thunderdome, Crocodile Dundee, Dead Calm.*

WEEKS, Jo, b. Melbourne, Vic, 1950. Films as continuity person include: *Winter of Our Dreams, Kitty and the Bagman, Far East, Melba* (mini-series).

WILLIAMSON, David, b. Melbourne, Vic, 1942. Films as writer include: *Don's Party, Gallipoli, The Year of Living Dangerously, Phar Lap, Travelling North.*

WILLIS, Pam, b. Hobart, Tas, 1948. Films as continuity person include: *Goodbye Paradise, Careful He Might Hear You, The Empty Beach, Travelling North.*

WINGROVE, John, b. Sydney, NSW, 1942. Films as art director include: *Careful He Might Hear You, For Love Alone, Mosquito Coast.*

Crew Roles

Animal Wrangler   In charge of finding, training and supervising animals used in filming.

Armourer   Someone licensed to carry firearms who is always present when guns or replica guns are used on set.

Arranger   Prepares and adapts previously written music for recording.

Art Department Coordinator   On a large film a Coordinator may be used to carry out some of the functions of the Art Director, particularly keeping the Art Department's accounts and organising the Department's personnel.

Art Department Runner   A driver who will be sent to collect or return items required by the Art Department.

Art Director   The Art Department's administrator. Responsible for the smooth running of the Art Department and keeping a check on the Art Department's budget. Facilitates the practical realisation of the Production Designer's concept.

Assistant Editor   Syncs up rushes, logs and files all the material coming from location and the laboratory, helps maintain the editing equipment, assists the editor in finding specific shots, re-winds spools of film and magnetic tape, etc.

Assistant Grip   Assists the Grip and Camera Departments.

Assistant Mixer   Frequently pre-mixes many of the tracks. Assists the Mixer during the final mix usually by riding (maintaining) the levels of the atmosphere and effects tracks, leaving the dialogue to the Mixer.

Assistant Sound Editor   Assists the Sound Editor. Helps locate specific recordings. Assists in laying up the sound tracks.

Associate Producer   This role varies markedly. May be a person carrying out most of the Production Manager's duties, or someone who is not directly involved in making the film but has some creative input. Sometimes used as a means of supplying writers, consultants, or crew members with a higher or additional salary.

Best Boy   The second in command to the Gaffer. A person experienced in film lighting who sets and adjusts lights under instruction from the Gaffer.

Boom Operator (Boom Swinger)   Sound crew member who manipulates the microphone, usually on a boom or fishpole. Directly responsible to the Sound Recordist. When radio microphones are in use, fits these onto the appropriate cast members. Generally assists the Sound Recordist.

Camera Assistant   On a large film (particularly where more than one camera is being used) an additional Camera Assistant may be used to help carry and maintain camera gear, assist the Clapper/Loader, or help with special gear such as a video split. On a small camera crew, the Camera Assistant will perform the functions of both Focus Puller and Clapper/Loader.

Camera Operator   Operates or manipulates the camera under instruction from the DOP and Director. Responsible for keeping the shots well composed and ensuring that nothing unwanted, such as a microphone, enters frame.

Carpenter (Chippy)   Builds sets and other constructions under the supervision of the Construction Manager.

Casting Consultant   Also known as a Casting Director. The person or company responsible for seeking out, recommending, and arranging interviews with prospective actors.

Catering   Provides meals for the cast and crew during filming.

Cinematographer   (*see* Director of Photography)

Clapper/Loader   Helps organise the camera gear. Loads the magazines with film stock and unloads the exposed film. Labels cans of exposed film with appropriate instructions for processing. Keeps a check of the takes and footage used and notes the print takes. Calls each shot and marks it with the clapper-board.

Composer   Composes original music for the film.

Construction Manager   Responsible for the construction crew (known colloquially as 'chippies'). Oversees all studio and location construction work such as the building of sets, and ensures that they are built on schedule.

Construction Runner   Purchases building materials for the construction crew, and generally assists them.

Continuity   The Editor's representative on set, and an aide to the Director. Times the script, keeps track of the coverage, and looks after the continuity details of props, wardrobe, performance, etc. Ensures that the various shots will cut together.

Costume Designer   Head of the Wardrobe Department. Designs all the costumes to be used in the film. Liaises with the Director, DOP, and Production Designer with regard to the look of the wardrobe.

Costume Supervisor   Second in charge of the Wardrobe Department. Coordinates the purchase and making of costumes.

Director   The person who vets the creative decisions of the scriptwriter and the other departments, dictates where the camera will be placed and how scenes will be shot, and guides the performances of the speaking cast. The Director also oversees the editing and mixing processes.

Director of Photography   (DOP, Dp, Lighting Cameraman, Cinematographer) The head of the Camera Department. Responsible for the film's image quality: lighting each shot, determining the exposure, deciding which filters to use. Will work with the Director and Camera Operator (though the DOP may also operate) in setting up and composing each shot.

Draughtsperson   Draws scale plans of the sets and/or props to be constructed, under instruction of the Production Designer, for use by the Construction Manager and/or Model Maker/Propsmaker.

Editor   The Picture Editor is the head of the Editing Department, and edits the picture with its attendant original dialogue tracks, until both s/he and the Director and/or Producer are satisfied with the result. This fine cut is then make available to the Sound Editors. Often the picture editor will lay up the music tracks as well.

Electrician   Sets and adjusts lights under instruction from the Gaffer and Best Boy.

Executive Producer   A person who is removed from the day-to-day business of the film but oversees the production as a whole. Often responsible for raising the finance and setting up the project. An Executive Producer may be involved in a number of projects at the same time.

Extras Casting   Chooses and books extras.

Fight Coordinator   Orchestrates and assists in directing fight sequences.

First Assistant Director   Schedules the film, aids the Director, and runs the set. The 'First' is responsible for ensuring that the film is shot on time and that filming proceeds smoothly and efficiently. The First also directs the extras.

Focus Puller   Using a tape measure, checks the distance between the subject and the camera, and maintains the required focus. When either the subject or the camera moves, this may require the focus to be adjusted or 'pulled'. Also threads the film into the camera with each magazine change, and changes lenses as required. Responsible for camera maintenance.

Gaffer   Head of the Electrics Department. Sets the lights and associated lighting equipment under instruction from the DOP. Generally provides all relevent lighting equipment: lamps, gels, cutters, stands, etc.

Generator Operator   Operates the Electrics Department's generator which provides electricity for lighting.

Grader (Colour Grader)   The employee of the laboratory who grades the film prior to answer printing.

Grip   Under instruction from the Key Grip, assists in setting up the dolly and crane shots, carrying camera gear, building platforms, constructing rigs, etc.

Hairdresser   Designs and maintains appropriate hair styles for the cast. Looks after hair continuity during shooting.

Hairdressing Assistant   Assists the Hairdresser when there is a large cast.

Key Grip   The Head of the Grips Department. Responsible for positioning the camera under instruction from the DOP and Camera Operator. Responsible for carrying out all dolly and crane shots, blacking out sets and locations, carrying gear, rigging the camera onto vehicles, building platforms, etc.

Lab Liaison   An employee of the laboratory who is charged with the responsibility of overseeing all the lab work required for a specific film.

Line Producer   A person who carries out the business functions of a producer during the making of the film, but does not shoulder responsibility for the creative decisions.

Location Manager   Scouts for appropriate locations, arranges for permission to use locations, and negotiates the terms for their use. Liaises with Local Councils, Police Department etc.

Make-up Artist   Designs and applies appropriate make-up to the cast. Maintains the correct make-up during shooting and looks after make-up continuity. Liaises with the Director, DOP, and Production Designer with regard to the look of the make-up. Often provides special effects make-up such as scars, wounds, etc. On a small cast film may also carry out the functions of Hairdresser.

Make-up Assistant   When a large cast is used, one or more Make-up Assistants will be employed to apply make-up to the cast under instruction from the Make-up Artist.

Mixer (Sound Mixer)   In the mixing theatre, adjusts the quality and levels of all the various sound tracks so that dialogue, music, effects, etc. all finish up at appropriate relative volumes.

Model Maker   This term may refer to someone who makes models or miniatures for filming, or it may be a person who makes models of sets prior to their construction.

Neg Matcher (Neg Cutter)   Matches every frame of the cut work-print with the original picture negative, and makes up the rolls of original film from which the prints or internegs will be struck.

Painter   Paints the sets.

Post-production Supervisor   Oversees the editing, sound mixing, and the laboratory work after the shoot. Basically a production manager for the post-production period.

Producer   Responsible for overseeing the entire production. Generally raises the finance, oversees expenditure priorities, assists in choosing key crew and principal cast, and ensures the original concept is being adhered to. Arranges distribution and assists in marketing.

Production Accountant   Looks after the financial accounts of the film or production company, and arranges payments for all concerned.

Production Coordinator   Works directly with the Production Manager in fulfilling the day-to-day business of the production office: giving cast or their agents the call times, booking equipment, arranging transport, etc.

Production Designer   The head of the Art Department. Responsible for the overall visual design of the sets (whether studio or location), set dressing, props, vehicles etc. Often oversees the 'look' of the wardrobe and make-up.

Production Manager   Responsible for ensuring that the budget is adhered to, negotiates contracts, engages crew members, and keeps the crew and set supplied with equipment and facilities.

Production Runner   A driver or courier for the production office.

Production Secretary   The Production Manager's secretary. Answers the telephone, types script ammendments and daily call sheets, etc. On a small film where there is no Production Coordinator, the Production Secretary will perform many of the Coordinator's duties.

Props Buyer   Purchases hand props and set dressings under instruction from the Production Designer and Art Director.

Props Maker   Constructs props. This person may also be used to make scale models of sets prior to construction.

Publicist   The person responsible for promotion and publicity of the film.

Safety Coordinator (Safety Officer).   Responsible for overseeing safety of the crew, cast, and stunt team. Liaises with the First Assistant Director, Stunt Coordinator, Special Effects Coordinator, Unit Nurse, and any other necessary personnel.

Safety Report Writer   All Australian films must have a Safety Report compiled by a suitably qualified person who has been approved by the Australian Theatrical and Amusement Employees Association and Actors Equity of Australia. On the basis of the script and discussions in pre-production with the First Assistant Director, and any other necessary crew, the consultant will advise on all matters pertaining to safety.

Scenic Artist   Paints sets, shoot-offs, murals, billboards, signs, etc. More of an artist than a painter.

Scriptwriter   The person who writes the screenplay.

Seamstress   Makes costumes to the designs of the Wardrobe Designer.

Second Assistant Director Provides the link between the production office and the set, looks after the cast, helps organise the extras, writes up the daily call sheet, and acts as an aide to the First.

Second Unit Director The person who directs shots or sequences which do not require the attention of the full crew — usually material not involving any speaking cast.

Second Unit Director of Photography (Second Unit Cameraman) A camera person hired to shoot and/or light material that falls into the second unit category (*see also* Second Unit Director)

Set Dresser Arranges the props and set dressing for each studio set and location prior to filming.

Sound Editor (Dubbing Editor) Lays up the various components of the sound in preparation for mixing. Cleans up the dialogue tracks, (this is sometimes the job of a specialist, known as a Dialogue Editor). Finds appropriate atmosphere and effects and lays them in sync with the picture.

Sound Recordist In charge of recording all necessary and available sound during the shoot. This includes dialogue, effects, and atmospheres. Monitors the recording levels, and generally supplies and maintains the necessary recording gear.

Special Effects Coordinator The person in charge of all special effects. Depending on the film's requirements, these may range from large pyrotechnics such as explosions, fire, and smoke, to creating wind and rain.

Special Effects Make-up Provides special make-up or prosthetic constructions for extraordinary visual effects such as monsters, major injuries, etc.

Special Effects Technician Sets and operates special effects under instruction from the Special Effects Coordinator.

Standby Props The Art Department's principal representative on set. Responsible for looking after all hand-props, and carrying out any last minute alterations to the set or location as requested by the Director or DOP. Responsible for the maintenance of the set and its dressings while the crew are working.

Standby Wardrobe The Wardrobe Department's representative on set. Dresses the cast, maintains the costumes, looks after wardrobe continuity on set.

Steadicam Operator   A Camera Operator brought in specifically to shoot set-ups involving Steadicam — a special body frame and rig designed for very steady hand-held shots.

Stills Photographer   Takes photographs for publicity purposes.

Storyboard Artist   A person hired to produce drawings that comprise the story board, a series of drawings like a cartoon strip depicting each shot to be filmed. This task will be carried out under detailed instruction from the Director who determines what each drawing (i.e. shot) will depict.

Stunt Coordinator   The person in charge of designing and supervising stunts. The Stunt Coordinator will quote a cost for all the stunt work, and choose the stunt team. S/he will then liaise with the Director, First Assistant Director, Special Effects Coordinator, Art Department and Safety Officer.

Stunt Double   A Stunt Person who is made up to resemble an actor in the film..

Stunt Person   A person who performs dangerous or potentially dangerous action under instruction from the Stunt Coordinator.

Third Assistant Director   Helps organise cast and extras, and acts as a gofer for the First and Second Assistant Directors.

Tutor   When using minors in the cast, a tutor must be present to assist them with their schoolwork when they are not required on set.

Unit Manager   Looks after facilities for the crew: parking of vehicles, providing space and power for make-up and wardrobe, organising toilets, setting up barricades, liaising with location owners, disposing of rubbish, etc. At times this job will overlap with the Location Manager and the Third Assistant Director.

Unit Nurse   Looks after the health of the crew and cast. Many films now employ a Nurse to be present throughout filming, whilst smaller budget films may simply engage a Nurse on specific days where health and safety are an issue such as days involving stunts and special effects.

Voice Coach   Assists cast members with their diction and/or accents. Generally employed to assist those actors who have had little or no formal training to improve their vocal delivery.

Glossary

(All definitions refer to common Australian usage.)

Action 1) Any movement or activity in front of the camera. 2) What the director says when s/he wishes the performances or activity in a given take to commence.

Action Vehicle Any vehicle which is featured in the on-screen action.

Adaptation A script based on another source.

Anamorphic Lens Used for very wide screen photography and projection, creating a deliberate horizontal distortion of the image. This compression enables a much wider aspect ratio to be 'squeezed' onto normal width film. The special lens for the projector spreads the image so that it is free from distortion.

Angle (Camera Angle) The position and direction from which a shot is taken by the camera. The angle determines from what vantage the audience will view the action.

Arc Light A carbon arc light is an extremely powerful, though heavy and cumbersome light, most often used for lighting large exteriors, particularly at night.

Answer Print The first trial print(s) presented by the laboratory for the customer's approval. Generally the first combined picture and sound print, with the picture correctly graded for density and colour, and the sound correctly synchronised.

Aspect Ratio The ratio of width to height of a projected picture image.

Assembly The initial piecing together of a film by the editor with all sequences in their correct script order. This may describe a stage prior to the 'rough cut', or it may be used as a term to denote 'rough cut'.

Atmosphere Track Background sounds used to flesh-out and enhance the soundtrack e.g. wind, traffic, birds, etc.

Auteur **Theory** A popular model of filmmaking which insists that the director is the principal author of his or her film, a concept championed by Francois Truffaut and André Bazin in the French film journal *Cahiers de Cinéma* during the 1950s.

Blacking Out Placing black material over light sources (such as windows, doorways, etc) to stop ambient light when shooting day-for-night interiors.

Block through An initial rehearsal of the action on set, in front of the crew, to establish the actors' movements and to facilitate discussion about the camera positions (i.e. set-ups).

Boom 1) An extending pole to which a microphone is attached. This is then held so as to extend above the actors as they speak. (Also known as a Fishpole). 2) A wheeled pedestal with a long arm mounted on the top, at the end of which a microphone is attached. Used for mikeing actors in studio situations, most commonly in television studios.

Budget 1) A breakdown of every possible cost in the making of a film. 2) The total cost of a film.

Burnt-out An area of the image (usually a window or doorway) which is lit and/or exposed to turn bright white, with the resultant loss of picture detail and colour.

Call (Call-time) The time at which each crew and cast member are required to be on set.

Call Sheet Prepared by the second assistant director under the supervision of the first assistant director, the call sheet gives all the relevent information for each day's shooting, such as: scene numbers to be shot, crew and cast call-times, directions to location, catering information, special requirements, etc.

Camera Crew The complete camera team: director of photography, camera operator, focus puller, and clapper/loader.

Camera Report A detailed account prepared each day by the clapper/loader listing the takes for each shot, the amount of film exposed, and instructions for the laboratory as to which takes to print and how they are to be printed.

Cast The performers appearing in the film.

Casting The process of choosing actors to play the roles.

Character A person in a film.

Characterisation All details of appearance and behaviour which define a given person in the story.

Cheat Changing the position of the cast, props or set dressing when switching camera angles. This may be necessary in order to place the camera, create a balanced composition in the frame, or avoid seeing an object or person in a given set-up. Usually positions are established in the master shot and may need to be cheated in cover shots.

Cherry picker Large mobile crane frequently hired by film crews to achieve very high angle or 'top' shots.

Clapper Board Also know as the slate. A hinged board which, when clapped together, provides the cue for the image and sound to be synchronised in the editing room. The slate contains written information denoting the production, the camera roll number, the shot number, and the take number.

Close-up (CU) A shot in which a person's head and shoulders or a small object fills the screen.

Closed Set A set in either the studio or on location that is not open to visitors. Usually refers to occasions when intimate scenes involving nudity are to be shot. Sometimes only a limited number of essential crew members are allowed on set in such instances.

Completion Guarantors —*see* Guarantors

Composition The way people and objects are positioned in the frame.

Contingency A specific percentage of the budget, usually ten per cent, to cover unexpected expenditures and rises in costs.

Coverage The choice of camera angles and shots used to complete a scene.

Cover Shots Any set-ups that could be used to inter-cut with the master shot.

Crane 1) Any pivoted arm system for raising the camera vertically in the air. 2) To move the camera vertically up or down as in a Crane Shot.

Credits List of who did what in a film's production. More often used to refer to the words appearing at the end of a film or End Credits. *See also* Titles.

Crossing The Line When the apparent geography of a scene is inadvertantly disturbed such that a character or object appears to be facing or moving in the wrong direction, the camera is said to have 'crossed the line'. (For a more detailed explanation, see the chapter on the continuity person.)

Cut 1) To change from one shot to another in editing. 2) A version of the edited film (rough cut, fine cut, etc). 3) What the Director calls when s/he wants the camera, sound and action to stop.

Cutaway In editing, a term to describe cutting from one shot to another in order to return to the first shot at a subsequent point. The intervening shot is of a different subject — it might be a close-up of an object such as a clock, for example.

Cutting Copy — *see* workprint.

Cutting Room The editor's place of work.

Cyclorama A large canvas screen attached to the floor which wraps around the back of a sound stage.

Daily Production Report Compiled by the production office and containing essential information about the day's filming and how the shoot is progressing, including: scenes/ screen-time shot; film stock used, shooting ratio, number of set-ups; hours worked by the crew and cast; progress to date; and any remarks regarding the day's events.

Day-For-Night Filming night scenes during daylight hours.

Depth of Field The distance between objects in the foreground and those in the background that are of acceptable sharpness of focus.

Developing That part of laboratory processing which makes visible the latent image of the exposed film.

Dialogue Track The sound track(s) that carries the dialogue, as opposed to the music track or effects track.

Dissolve An optical effect whereby the end of one shot overlaps with the beginning of the next shot so that a gradual transition occurs between the two images.

Dolly 1) A wheeled device for physically moving the camera and camera operator, for the purpose of tracking or dolly shots. The dolly may travel on tracks (rails), on boards, or on the ground if the surface is sufficiently smooth. 2) Any shot involving the use of a dolly is known as a dolly shot. Thus one can dolly in or dolly out relative to the subject in frame.

Dupe Short for duplicate. A new dupe negative (or internegative) may be made from the original negative. A dupe of the cut workprint (also known as a slashprint) may be made for the sound editor to use.

Editing 1) The process of selecting, arranging and assembling the pieces of film and the sound track. 2) Script editing involves rationalising, and 'tightening up' a script to make it more dramatically coherent and effective.

Emulsion The part of the film which reacts to light (dispersions of light-sensitive materials in a colloidal medium, usually gelatin, carried as a thin layer on film base).

Exhibitor The owner of the theatre in which the film is being screened.

Exposed Film Film that has been exposed to light i.e. film that has been shot, but not processed.

Exposure The amount of light allowed to reach the film.

Exterior Any action or filming which takes place out of doors.

Extras Actors used in the background behind the principal action or in crowd scenes, under direction from the first assistant director, and who do not speak dialogue except *en mass*.

Fade 1) Where the image goes to black or appears from black. 2) Where a sound disappears gradually.

Favouring Framing a shot to favour an actor thus ensuring that they are dominant in the composition.

Feature 1) A full length film usually of 90 minutes or more duration. 2) To make something important in the film is to 'feature' it.

Fill Light Secondary lights used to lessen the directness of the key light.

Film Stock — *see* raw stock.

Filters Coloured or clear pieces of glass or gelatin placed over the camera lens which absorb a particular part of the colour spectrum or diffuse the light.

Final Cut The point at which the edited image is 'locked-off' and will no longer be tampered with, so that track-laying and mixing can occur. (An important aspect of the director's contract will be the determination of whether s/he has the 'final cut' — in other words, the last say on the form and content).

Final Mix All the sound elements (dialogue, music, effects) combined in their final mixed state.

Fine Cut A refined, edited version of the film which precedes track laying.

First Draft The first complete version of a script.

Fishpole An extending pole to which a microphone is attached. (Also referred to as a boom.)

Flashback A shot, scene, or sequence which intercuts with the film's narrative to reveal an event which happened prior to the time frame of the narrative at that particular point in the movie.

Floor The place where the main unit crew is filming.

Flop-Over To turn the film over so that the lateral direction of the action is reversed i.e. right-to-left becomes left-to-right.

Focus To adjust the lens to ensure that the subject appears crisp and sharp. Changing the focus during a shot is known as 'pulling focus'.

Fog Filter A filter placed in front of the camera lens which creates a soft-edge image.

Foley Studio A recording studio used for recording post-sync sound effects in time with a screened image (e.g. footsteps, scraping, punches, etc.).

Follow Shot A shot in which the camera moves independently, in time with the subject, and goes where the subject goes.

Footage Any length of film, usually expressed in feet or frames. 16 frames = one foot of 35 mm film.

Frame 1) Each separate, individual image of the film. In the cinema these are projected at a rate of 14 frames per second. 2) The boundaries of the image. Anything inside this area is said to be in-frame, and beyond is out of frame. 3) To frame a shot is to set the composition by positioning all the elements within the boundaries of image.

Freeze 1) A laboratory process whereby one frame of the image is repeated for a given length of film, giving the appearance that the image is frozen, or static for the duration of the freeze. 2) What the first assistant director may call at the end of a take immediately after the director has called 'cut'. This signifies to the actors that they are to hold their positions so that the Focus Puller can check the focus.

Gate Check (Checking the Gate) Looking into the camera's gate (where the film runs through directly behind the lens) after each set-up to ensure there is no foreign matter or film scrapings that may have appeared on the image.

Glass Diffusion Loose term referring to any glass filter placed in front of the lens which will alter or diffuse the light and subsequent image.

Grading A laboratory process whereby the light intensity and colour of each shot is adjusted so that the film gains uniformity in its release print.

Guarantors (Completion Guarantors) Engaged by the financiers to ensure the film is completed on budget.

Guide Track A sound track of unavoidable sub-standard quality, recorded when it is impossible to avoid unwanted sounds, e.g. recording dialogue near a noisy building site. It is used as a guide in editing for post-synchronisation.

Hand-held Shooting with the camera being entirely supported by the camera operator (usually by resting it on his/her shoulder), and thus without the aid of a tripod or dolly.

Hand Props Objects which are scripted for specific use by the actors within scenes, e.g. guns, newspapers, cigarette lighters, etc.

High-angle Shot A camera angle from a high position looking down on the action.

High key A lighting style in which light, highly illuminated areas predominate (as can be found in most comedy pictures for example).

Insert A shot of short duration, usually a descriptive close-up, which cuts into a sequence to highlight some specific action or detail.

Intercut To cut between two or more different sequences of action giving the impression that they are happening concurrently.

Interior Any action or filming which takes place indoors.

Jump-cut A cut which takes place abruptly and draws attention to itself.

Key Light A light which provides the major source of illumination for the subject.

Kill To turn off. Usually in reference to lamps.

Lab (Laboratory) The place where film is developed, processed and printed.

Lab Report (Rushes Report) After processing and printing each day's rushes (usually overnight), the laboratory will view them and report on any technical problems that they perceive e.g. if the film is scratched or damaged in any way.

Lens The glass and its casing that focuses the image onto the film.

Lightflex A device which is mounted in front of the camera's lens, which adds light to the overall image during shooting. The result is more detail in the shadow areas of the image and colour toning reminiscent of period photography.

Lightmeter Used by the DOP to measure the intensity of the light: to ensure that the film is correctly exposed, to estimate the way light and dark areas in the frame will affect the film emulsion, and to ensure that there is continuity in the lighting.

Location Any locale used for shooting that is not in a studio or sound stage.

Location Survey A visit in pre-production by key crew members to the locations that will be used for filming. (Also known as a location recce.)

Locked-off 1) When the picture is said to be locked-off it means that the image has reached its final length and will not be tampered with any further. This means that the sound editor can lay up sound tracks that will be the same length as the image from the first frame to the last. Thus all the sound tracks will remain in sync. 2) When a camera is locked-off it is secured so that it will not move during the take.

Long Shot A relative term generally referring to any shot which records a verticle area equivalent to an adult from head to toe, or larger.

Louma Crane French-made crane which will raise the camera, Camera Operator, and Focus Puller to 23 feet above the ground.

Low key A lighting style in which dark, shadowy areas predominate (as can be found in most horror pictures, for example).

Magazine The removable part of the camera which contains the film.

Main Unit The principal crew which films the major proportion of the material.

Master Control The part of a TV station which cues up and monitors all material going to air.

Master Shot A single set-up, usually a fairly wide shot, which incorporates all the action for a given scene. It then becomes a point of reference for all further coverage in the scene.

Mid Shot A relative term sometimes used as a synonym for medium shot, and sometimes for a loose close-up. Generally a mid-shot will frame a person from the middle of their chest, but may be as wide as to frame the subject from the waist up.

Medium Shot Half-way between a close-up and a long shot. Generally a person will be framed from the waist up. Again the term is relative.

Mix Combining separate sound tracks laid up by the sound editor into a single sound track using the expertise of one or more mixers.

Montage A series of consecutive shots that cut together to tell a story within the story, or denote a passage of time.

Mute Filming without recording sound. (Also referred to as M.O.S.)

Nagra The most widely used brand of self-contained sound recorder used in filmmaking.

Negative Any processed film that possesses a negative picture image (i.e. opposite image tones) of the subject to which the film was exposed.

On-mike When the subject being recorded is in a direct line with the microphone (as opposed to off-mike, when the subject is not being recorded effectively).

Opticals Post-production visual effects created in the laboratory e.g. dissolves, fades, wipes, and titles.

Original Screenplay A script written specifically for the screen and not adapted from any other source.

Outline The bare bones of a script. A brief scene-by-scene narrative description including short character sketches.

Pan Any side-to-side or horizontal movement of the camera on its axis.

Panavision Trademark of a specific motion picture camera system often used in shooting feature films.

Performance The work done by an actor in the film.

Pick-up 1) A shot required to be filmed after the scene in which it will be used has already been shot i.e. a shot required to complete or enhance the existing coverage. 2) If a long take is useable only in part, it may be decided (to save footage) to only run part of the action on the next take. Thus one 'picks up' part of the action.

Picture Negative The processed, exposed film negative from which all positive prints or internegatives are struck.

Point-of-view (POV) A shot filmed to appear to be seen from a specific character's eyes.

Post-production The period following principal photography and leading up to release printing i.e. editing, track-laying, mixing, scoring, neg-cutting, grading.

Post-sync Recording the sound separately, and fitting it to an existing image. Usually the term is used to refer to recording and synchronising voice tracks after the image has been cut.

Pre-production The period of preparation before principal photography begins.

Pre-mix A mix of several sound tracks onto one single track to make the final mix more manageable e.g. one may pre-mix the atmosphere tracks, or the dialogue tracks, etc.

Pre-sale A distribution guarantee or television sale which occurs prior to production.

Principals The members of the cast who are the main featured actors.

Principal Photography The period of filming that involves the Main Unit. In other words, the main filming period.

Print The positive image struck from the exposed negative film.

Print Take Any take which the director wishes to have printed for subsequent perusal and possible use in editing. (To reduce laboratory costs, not all takes of each set-up are printed as workprint in the lab — only those which the director stipulates.)

Processing A generic term for developing and printing film.

Radio Mike A small microphone which can be worn and concealed beneath clothing, and which transmits its signal to a small radio receiver connected to the sound recorder. Thus speaking cast who cannot be effectively recorded using a microphone on a boom due to either their action, or the framing of the shot (e.g. a very wide shot), can be fitted with radio mikes. However, they are not generally favoured by sound recordists due to their poor dynamic range and their fallibility.

Ratio — *see* Shooting Ratio

Raw Stock Unexposed film, or unused sound tapes.

Redhead A small lamp used in film lighting.

Reel A spool of film or sound tape. In 35 mm film, each reel of film for projection and storage runs between 900 and 1,000 feet — around 10 minutes of screentime.

Release Print A composite print containing the final image and sound suitable for screening.

Re-shooting Filming something that has already been shot either for technical or aesthetic reasons.

Reveal A shot that widens out or pulls back to show something that was not visible at the beginning of the shot.

Reverse Sometimes erroniously called a 'reversal'. A shot taken from an angle approximately 180 degrees from the preceding shot e.g. when two actors are facing one another.

Re-voicing Replacing the voice of an actor with the voice of another actor.

Rig Shot A set-up where the camera is attached to a rig constructed by the Grip Department e.g. when a camera must be attached to the side of a moving vehicle.

Rights 1) The copyright of a literary work upon which a screenplay may be based. 2) The copyright of a film i.e. a legal agreement to use the film for screening.

Rock and Roll Term used to describe film projection capable of both forward and reverse operation. Sound mixing theatres employ this process extensively to go back and forth over the same sequence during the sound mix.

Roll 1) A roll or spool of film or sound tape. 2) What the first assistant director may call when signalling for the camera and/or sound recorder to turn on. — *see also* Turn Over.

Rough Cut An edited assembly of all the scenes in their approximate order, but without any fine-tuning to the cuts.

Rushes The shots completed on each day of filming are processed overnight at the laboratory, synced up with the sound in the editing room, and screened after wrap on the following day. Rushes are thus the day's filming which is 'rushed' through the lab. In the USA they are known as dailies.

Scene A script is broken into individual scenes, each of which consists of a specific piece of action occurring at a given time at a given location. Whenever the location changes or there is a leap in time it becomes a new scene and is allocated a new scene number.

Scene Number Each scene in the script is allocated with a scene number so that all the scenes may be identified by their number. The average feature script has between 100 and 150 scenes.

Schedule (Shooting Schedule) An arrangement of scenes to be shot on each shooting day. A printed shooting schedule will detail locations, cast requirements, essential props, vehicles, livestock, and any other requirements for each scene to be shot each day.

Screenplay The written script, divided into scenes, and conforming to the standard rules for layout, upon which a film is based.

Screen Test An audition which is recorded on film or videotape.

Second Unit A small crew used to pick up shots which do not require the principal cast and which can be directed by a second unit director.

Sequence Usually this refers to a group of scenes which form part of an identifiable larger unit of the script i.e. a group of scenes which cut together to create a specific sequence of events in the same script time frame.

Set 1) The place where the film crew is working. 2) A construction in a studio or sound stage.

Set Dressing Any items of set decoration such as furniture, props, drapery, carpets, etc., which are not usually specifically designated in the script.

Set-up The specific arrangement of camera, actors, lights, etc., which culminates in a series of takes. Each time the camera is moved to a new position for each shot it is known as a new set-up.

Shoot 1) The process of actually filming is known as shooting. To shoot something is to film it. 2) The Shoot is the period of time between pre-production and post-production when filming takes place.

Shoot-off A flat, ceiling piece, diorama, or painted landscape, etc., which can be positioned when the camera sees beyond the confines of the set e.g. through a window, doorway, or off the top of the set.

Shooting Ratio The ratio of the amount of film actually exposed to the amount of film required in the final print.

Shooting Schedule — *see* Schedule.

Shooting Script The final version of the script ready to go before the camera.

Shot A specific camera position with its requisite action, lighting and camera movement. There may be a number of takes of each shot. (This term is largely synonymous with the term set-up).

Shutter A rotating fan-shaped blade which prevents light from reaching the film while it is in motion from one frame to the next.

Shutter Speed The speed at which the film passes through the camera. Most film is shot at 24 frames-per-second. However film for TV is often shot at 25 frames-per-second as this is the speed which film is projected when transferred to video.

Single A shot in which there is one person in frame.

16 mm A gauge of filmstock and its associated equipment: 16 millimetres referring to the width of the film itself. 16 mm is a professional gauge with is used extensively in documentary film-making, and in Australia it is generally used when shooting TV drama on film.

Slate 1) The hinged board which, when clapped together, provides the cue for the image and the sound to be synchronised in the editing room. The slate contains written information denoting the production, the camera roll number, the shot number, and the take number. 2) Another term for take.

Sound Stage A studio space built specifically for filming purposes with a lighting grid, cyclorama, and which is effectively sound-proofed against any external noise.

Stand-in A person who replaces a principal actor for the purpose of technical adjustments such as lighting, camera placement, etc. A stand-in may also be used for filming when the actor will not be recognised e.g. in extreme wide shots.

Steadicam A special camera mount and body harness which is worn by a camera operator and allows for very steady shots as the operator moves.

Stock Unexposed film or unused sound tapes.

Storyboard A series of drawings that show each individual shot planned to cover a sequence or an entire film.

Storyline The sequence of events and plot structure which make up the narrative of a script.

Striking 1) When referring to a set, to strike means to remove all dressing or dismantle a studio construction. 2) When referring to a camera set-up, striking means to remove the camera and lights prior to moving on to the next set-up.

Stripboard (Production Stripboard) The first assistant director's tool for scheduling. Strips of coloured cardboard containing coded information for each scene are rearranged in a large concertina folder.

Studio In Australia, any large space in which sets are constructed for filming is known as a studio. This may be either an appropriate sound stage or merely a factory space.

Stunt A dangerous or potentially dangerous action to be performed by a stunt person.

Sync An abbreviation for synchronisation. When in sync, the image and sound coincide properly. When out of sync, they are mis-matched. Syncing of rushes means matching the film image to the magnetic sound using the slate (or clapper-board) as a cue.

Take A single, continuous piece of film from when the camera turns on until it turns off again. There may be several takes of any given shot or set-up. Separate performances when recording wild sound are also known as takes.

Telemovie (Telefeature) A feature-length film made for distribution through television and not for cinema release.

10B(A) A federal government scheme which allowed investors in certified Australian films to tax concessions on their investment. Initially established at a rate of 150% of the investment in December 1980, this was subsequently reduced to 133% in August 1983, and again reduced to 120% in September 1985. In May 1988, when the government announced its intention to establish a film bank, 10B(A) was lowered to a flat 100% of the investment.

35 mm A gauge of film stock and its associated equipment: 35 millimetres refers to the width of the film. It is used for shooting films intended for theatrical release, and also many commercials for TV due to its superior image quality.

Tilt A vertical or up and down movement of the camera on its axis.

Titles Words on the screen denoting the title of the film and who did what in its production. More often used to refer to the words at the beginning of the film or head titles.

Top Shot An angle looking straight down from on top of the subject.

Track 1) A system of moving the camera using a dolly. The dolly may move along metal rails (also known as tracks), or on boards, or along smooth ground to create a tracking shot (a.k.a. a dolly shot). 2) An abbreviation of sound track, being the audio component of the film.

Track Laying Positioning the separate audio elements (dialogue, effects, music, etc.) onto individual rolls which are in sync with the image, in preparation for the sound mix.

Turnaround The amount of time between wrap on one day and call on the next. The Australian Theatrical and Amusement Employees Association's award for film crews stipulates that the minimum turnaround should be 10 hours.

Turn-over What the first assistant director calls when signalling for the camera and sound recorder to switch on for the take. (An alternative term for roll.)

Two Shot A shot with two people in frame.

Video Split A device which allows for the image through the film camera to be relayed onto a video monitor, which can also be used to record each take.

Viewfinder (Director's Viewfinder) A small device which can be looked through to simulate various lens sizes on a camera. Used as a tool by the director, and sometimes the DOP, to determine what lens to use to cover an angle.

Voice Over (V/O) Literally, voice over the picture: the speaker is either not clearly visible, or not present in the image, yet can be heard e.g. running a conversation occurring inside a moving vehicle over a wide shot of the vehicle travelling down the street. A narration is also a voice over.

Widescreen General term for the most common form of film presentation in which the picture shown has an aspect ratio greater than 1.33:1.

Wild Lines Dialogue recorded independently of the camera. If the sound recordist is not happy about the quality of the recording on a certain line, speech or work, s/he may ask an actor to do a 'wild track'. This means that the necessary dialogue will be recorded in a number of variations so that it can be juggled into place by the sound editor to match the appropriate image.

Wild Sound Any sound recorded independently, and therefore not in sync with, the camera. Also known as a wild track.

Workprint Also known as the cutting copy. A positive print struck from the original picture negative. The workprint is what the editor will use during the editing process, so that the original negative can be kept secure and unmarked. Eventually, the cut workprint will be matched with the picture negative so that answer prints and release prints can be made.

Workshopping An intensive rehearsal period where the actors develop their characterisations. Often changes to the script are made as a result of this rehearsal also.

Wrap 1) The completion of each day's filming. 2) The completion of principal photography. 3) A general term used to refer to packing gear away or releasing artists and/or crew members from their work on a given day.

Wrap Shot The last set-up on each shooting day.

Zoom The image is progressively made larger or smaller through the use of a lens with variable focal length.

Index

A page reference in **bold** type is the principal reference to a topic.

ALSO FROM CURRENCY PRESS

THE SCREENING OF AUSTRALIA VOLS. I AND II
Susan Dermody and Elizabeth Jacka.

A definitive study of the Australian film industry. Volume I analyses the revived Australian cinema from 1970 to the present, covering government and union policies, and the patterns of subsidy and distribution. Volume II, through a detailed study of over two hundred films, provides a lively commentary on the direction and nature of Australian film. Often contentious, this thoroughly researched volume provides new material for debate as the industry faces new economic pressures. Contains filmography, and 52 B/W photographs.

AMERICAN DREAMS: AUSTRALIAN MOVIES
Peter Hamilton and Sue Mathews.

The impact upon American audiences of Australian movies has been startling. Critics, directors, producers and writers on both sides heap praise and scorn upon the films and those who make them. *American Dreams: Australian Movies* documents these witty, warring opinions and gives new insights into the traps and triumphs of working in the international film market.

AN AUSTRALIAN FILM READER
Albert Moran and Tom O'Regan.

Divided into four parts covering Early Cinema, Documentary Hopes, Renaissance of the Feature and Alternative Cinema, the *Reader* provides some of the most lucid commentary on this area of our national culture, with fifty extended articles from the most authoritative writers in their field.

For more information contact:
Currency Press
P.O. Box 452
Paddington 2021 NSW
Australia